International Institutions and the Political Economy of Integration

Integrating National Economies: Promise and Pitfalls

Barry Bosworth (Brookings Institution) and Gur Ofer (Hebrew University)
Reforming Planned Economies in an Integrating World Economy

Ralph C. Bryant (Brookings Institution)
International Coordination of National Stabilization Policies

Susan M. Collins (Brookings Institution/Georgetown University)
Distributive Issues: A Constraint on Global Integration

Richard N. Cooper (Harvard University)
Environment and Resource Policies for the World Economy

Ronald G. Ehrenberg (Cornell University)
Labor Markets and Integrating National Economies

Barry Eichengreen (University of California, Berkeley)
International Monetary Arrangements for the 21st Century

Mitsuhiro Fukao (Bank of Japan)
Financial Integration, Corporate Governance, and the Performance of Multinational Companies

Stephan Haggard (University of California, San Diego)
Developing Nations and the Politics of Global Integration

Richard J. Herring (University of Pennsylvania) and Robert E. Litan (Department of Justice/Brookings Institution)
Financial Regulation in the Global Economy

Miles Kahler (University of California, San Diego)
International Institutions and the Political Economy of Integration

Anne O. Krueger (Stanford University)
Trade Policies and Developing Nations

Robert Z. Lawrence (Harvard University)
Regionalism, Multilateralism, and Deeper Integration

Sylvia Ostry (University of Toronto) and Richard R. Nelson (Columbia University)
Techno-Nationalism and Techno-Globalism: Conflict and Cooperation

Robert L. Paarlberg (Wellesley College/Harvard University)
Leadership Abroad Begins at Home: U.S. Foreign Economic Policy after the Cold War

Peter Rutland (Wesleyan University)
Russia, Eurasia, and the Global Economy

F. M. Scherer (Harvard University)
Competition Policies for an Integrated World Economy

Susan L. Shirk (University of California, San Diego)
How China Opened Its Door: The Political Success of the PRC's Foreign Trade and Investment Reforms

Alan O. Sykes (University of Chicago)
Product Standards for Internationally Integrated Goods Markets

Akihiko Tanaka (Institute of Oriental Culture, University of Tokyo)
The Politics of Deeper Integration: National Attitudes and Policies in Japan

Vito Tanzi (International Monetary Fund)
Taxation in an Integrating World

William Wallace (St. Antony's College, Oxford University)
Regional Integration: The West European Experience

Miles Kahler

International
Institutions and
the Political Economy
of Integration

THE BROOKINGS INSTITUTION
Washington, D.C.

Library of Congress Cataloging-in-Publication data:
Kahler, Miles 1949–
International institutions and the political economy of integration/
Miles Kahler
p. cm.—(Integrating national economies)
Includes bibliographical references and index.
ISBN 0-8157-4822-1 (alk. paper).—ISBN 0-8157-4821-3 (alk. paper pbk.)
1. International economic integration.   2. International economic relations.
3. International finance.   I. Title.   II. Series.
HF1418.5.K34   1995
337.1—dc20   94-5148
                                                                  CIP

9 8 7 6 5 4 3 2 1

The paper used in this publication meets the minimum requirements of
American National Standard for Information Sciences—Permanence of Paper
for Printed Library Materials, ANSI Z39.48-1984

Typeset in Plantin

Composition by Princeton Editorial Associates
Princeton, New Jersey

Printed by R. R. Donnelley and Sons Co.
Harrisonburg, Virginia

Foreword

B Y definition international economic integration occurs among nation states. National leaders thus have a strong interest in managing integration to enhance national economic welfare and to satisfy their domestic constituencies. International institutions can play a key role in this environment, encouraging national governments to manage conflicts that arise from the real or perceived effects of economic integration. Indeed, new and revived international institutions have developed with economic integration at the global and the regional levels.

Miles Kahler analyzes how these institutions evolve with international economic change. At the global level, the divergent paths of the General Agreement on Tariffs and Trade (GATT) and the International Monetary Fund (IMF) illustrate how economic integration can undermine some international institutions and strengthen others. The open and flexible architecture of GATT was able to absorb an emerging agenda of behind-the-border issues. Increased financial integration ultimately undermined the Bretton Woods exchange rate system.

Regional institutions reveal even more dramatically the tension between national desires to maintain policy autonomy and, at the same time, benefit from intensified economic exchange. The European Union, the most centralized and strongest of regional institutions, constantly redraws the lines between regional and national policies. The United States, Canada, and Mexico originally designed NAFTA as a limited pact with modest institutional ambitions. They must now decide whether and how to widen the scope of agreed policies and enlarge NAFTA to a hemispheric free trade agreement. In the Pacific, the highly successful GATT-plus agreement between

Australia and New Zealand has been accompanied by little institution building, and the Asian partners of the United States in Asia-Pacific Economic Cooperation (APEC) have made clear that formal institutionalization is not high on their agenda.

In short, no single institutional model guarantees successful international collaboration. Rapid international economic change, domestic political demands, and the changing boundaries of knowledge reward institutions that are flexible and decentralized. Furthermore, international collaboration may be sustained by institutions that do not have great strength, clear rules, or centralized enforcement powers.

Miles Kahler is senior fellow at the Council on Foreign Relations and professor of international relations at the Graduate School of International Relations and Pacific Studies, University of California, San Diego. The author did much of the research and writing for this book at the Graduate School of International Relations and Pacific Studies, and he completed the final editing of the work at the Council on Foreign Relations. He is grateful to both institutions. He also thanks William Aceves, Steven Schwartz, and Timothy Johnson for research assistance. The Pacific Rim Research Program of the University of California generously supported this research. He also thanks Robert O. Keohane as well as Ralph Bryant and the participants in a Brookings review conference for their helpful comments on the first draft of this book.

Princeton Editorial Associates edited the manuscript and prepared the index. David Bearce verified the factual content of the manuscript.

Funding for the project came from the Center for Global Partnership of the Japan Foundation, the Curry Foundation, the Ford Foundation, the Korea Foundation, the Tokyo Club Foundation for Global Studies, the United States-Japan Foundation, and the Alex C. Walker Educational and Charitable Foundation. The author and Brookings are grateful for their support.

The views expressed in this book are those of the authors and should not be ascribed to any of the persons or organizations mentioned or acknowledged above, or to the trustees, officers, or staff members of the Brookings Institution.

BRUCE K. MACLAURY
President

March 1995
Washington, D.C.

Contents

Preface to the Studies on Integrating National Economies

ECONOMIC interdependence among nations has increased sharply in the past half century. For example, while the value of total production of industrial countries increased at a rate of about 9 percent a year on average between 1964 and 1992, the value of the exports of those nations grew at an average rate of 12 percent, and lending and borrowing across national borders through banks surged upward even more rapidly at 23 percent a year. This international economic interdependence has contributed to significantly improved standards of living for most countries. Continuing international economic integration holds out the promise of further benefits. Yet the increasing sensitivity of national economies to events and policies originating abroad creates dilemmas and pitfalls if national policies and international cooperation are poorly managed.

The Brookings Project on Integrating National Economies, of which this study is a component, focuses on the interplay between two fundamental facts about the world at the end of the twentieth century. First, the world will continue for the foreseeable future to be organized politically into nation-states with sovereign governments. Second, increasing economic integration among nations will continue to erode differences among national economies and undermine the autonomy of national governments. The project explores the opportunities and tensions arising from these two facts.

Scholars from a variety of disciplines have produced twenty-one studies for the first phase of the project. Each study examines the heightened competition between national political sovereignty and increased cross-border economic integration. This preface identifies background themes and issues common to all the studies and provides a brief overview of the project as a whole.[1]

Increasing World Economic Integration

Two underlying sets of causes have led nations to become more closely intertwined. First, technological, social, and cultural changes have sharply reduced the effective economic distances among nations. Second, many of the government policies that traditionally inhibited cross-border transactions have been relaxed or even dismantled.

The same improvements in transportation and communications technology that make it much easier and cheaper for companies in New York to ship goods to California, for residents of Strasbourg to visit relatives in Marseilles, and for investors in Hokkaido to buy and sell shares on the Tokyo Stock Exchange facilitate trade, migration, and capital movements spanning nations and continents. The sharply reduced costs of moving goods, money, people, and information underlie the profound economic truth that technology has made the world markedly smaller.

New communications technology has been especially significant for financial activity. Computers, switching devices, and telecommunications satellites have slashed the cost of transmitting information internationally, of confirming transactions, and of paying for transactions. In the 1950s, for example, foreign exchange could be bought and sold only during conventional business hours in the initiating party's time zone. Such transactions can now be carried out instantaneously twenty-four hours a day. Large banks pass the management of their worldwide foreign-exchange positions around the globe from one branch to another, staying continuously ahead of the setting sun.

Such technological innovations have increased the knowledge of potentially profitable international exchanges and of economic opportunities abroad. Those developments, in turn, have changed consumers' and producers' tastes. Foreign goods, foreign vacations, foreign financial investments—virtually anything from other nations—have lost some of their exotic character.

1. A complete list of authors and study titles is included at the beginning of this volume, facing the title page.

Although technological change permits increased contact among nations, it would not have produced such dramatic effects if it had been countermanded by government policies. Governments have traditionally taxed goods moving in international trade, directly restricted imports and subsidized exports, and tried to limit international capital movements. Those policies erected "separation fences" at the borders of nations. From the perspective of private sector agents, separation fences imposed extra costs on cross-border transactions. They reduced trade and, in some cases, eliminated it. During the 1930s governments used such policies with particular zeal, a practice now believed to have deepened and lengthened the Great Depression.

After World War II, most national governments began—sometimes unilaterally, more often collaboratively—to lower their separation fences, to make them more permeable, or sometimes even to tear down parts of them. The multilateral negotiations under the auspices of the General Agreement on Trade and Tariffs (GATT)—for example, the Kennedy Round in the 1960s, the Tokyo Round in the 1970s, and most recently the protracted negotiations of the Uruguay Round, formally signed only in April 1994—stand out as the most prominent examples of fence lowering for trade in goods. Though contentious and marked by many compromises, the GATT negotiations are responsible for sharp reductions in at-the-border restrictions on trade in goods and services. After the mid-1980s a large number of developing countries moved unilaterally to reduce border barriers and to pursue outwardly oriented policies.

The lowering of fences for financial transactions began later and was less dramatic. Nonetheless, by the 1990s government restrictions on capital flows, especially among the industrial countries, were much less important and widespread than at the end of World War II and in the 1950s.

By shrinking the economic distances among nations, changes in technology would have progressively integrated the world economy even in the absence of reductions in governments' separation fences. Reductions in separation fences would have enhanced interdependence even without the technological innovations. Together, these two sets of evolutionary changes have reinforced each other and strikingly transformed the world economy.

Changes in the Government of Nations

Simultaneously with the transformation of the global economy, major changes have occurred in the world's political structure. First, the number of governmental decisionmaking units in the world has expanded markedly, and political power has been diffused more broadly among them. Rising nationalism and, in some areas, heightened ethnic tensions have accompanied that increasing political pluralism.

The history of membership in international organizations documents the sharp growth in the number of independent states. For example, only 44 nations participated in the Bretton Woods conference of July 1944, which gave birth to the International Monetary Fund. But by the end of 1970, the IMF had 118 member nations. The number of members grew to 150 by the mid-1980s and to 178 by December 1993. Much of this growth reflects the collapse of colonial empires. Although many nations today are small and carry little individual weight in the global economy, their combined influence is considerable, and their interests cannot be ignored as easily as they were in the past.

A second political trend, less visible but equally important, has been the gradual loss of the political and economic hegemony of the United States. Immediately after World War II, the United States by itself accounted for more than one-third of world production. By the early 1990s the U.S. share had fallen to about one-fifth. Concurrently, the political and economic influence of the European colonial powers continued to wane, and the economic significance of nations outside Europe and North America, such as Japan, Korea, Indonesia, China, Brazil, and Mexico, increased. A world in which economic power and influence are widely diffused has displaced a world in which one or a few nations effectively dominated international decisionmaking.

Turmoil and the prospect of fundamental change in the formerly centrally planned economies compose a third factor causing radical changes in world politics. During the era of central planning, governments in those nations tried to limit external influences on their economies. Now leaders in the formerly planned economies are trying to adopt reforms modeled on Western capitalist principles. To the extent that these efforts succeed, those nations will increase their economic involvement with the rest of the world. Political and economic alignments among the Western industrialized nations will be forced to adapt.

Governments and scholars have begun to assess these three trends, but their far-reaching ramifications will not be clear for decades.

Dilemmas for National Policies

Cross-border economic integration and national political sovereignty have increasingly come into conflict, leading to a growing mismatch between the economic and political structures of the world. The effective domains of economic markets have come to coincide less and less with national governmental jurisdictions.

When the separation fences at nations' borders were high, governments and citizens could sharply distinguish "international" from "domestic" policies. International policies dealt with at-the-border barriers, such as tariffs and quotas, or responded to events occurring abroad. In contrast, domestic policies were concerned with everything behind the nation's borders, such as competition and antitrust rules, corporate governance, product standards, worker safety, regulation and supervision of financial institutions, environmental protection, tax codes, and the government's budget. Domestic policies were regarded as matters about which nations were sovereign, to be determined by the preferences of the nation's citizens and its political institutions, without regard for effects on other nations.

As separation fences have been lowered and technological innovations have shrunk economic distances, a multitude of formerly neglected differences among nations' domestic policies have become exposed to international scrutiny. National governments and international negotiations must thus increasingly deal with "deeper"—behind-the-border—integration. For example, if country A permits companies to emit air and water pollutants whereas country B does not, companies that use pollution-generating methods of production will find it cheaper to produce in country A. Companies in country B that compete internationally with companies in country A are likely to complain that foreign competitors enjoy unfair advantages and to press for international pollution standards.

Deeper integration requires analysis of the economic and the political aspects of virtually all nonborder policies and practices. Such issues have already figured prominently in negotiations over the evolution of the European Community, over the Uruguay Round of GATT negotiations, over the North American Free Trade Agreement (NAFTA), and over the bilateral economic relationships between Japan and the United States. Future debates about behind-the-border policies will occur with increasing frequency and prove at least as complex and contentious as the past negotiations regarding at-the-border restrictions.

Tensions about deeper integration arise from three broad sources: cross-border spillovers, diminished national autonomy, and challenges to political sovereignty.

Cross-Border Spillovers

Some activities in one nation produce consequences that spill across borders and affect other nations. Illustrations of these spillovers abound. Given the impact of modern technology of banking and securities markets in creating interconnected networks, lax rules in one nation erode the ability of all other nations to enforce banking and securities rules and to deal with fraudulent transactions. Given the rapid diffusion of knowledge, science and technology policies in one nation generate knowledge that other nations can use without full payment. Labor market policies become matters of concern to other nations because workers migrate in search of work; policies in one nation can trigger migration that floods or starves labor markets elsewhere. When one nation dumps pollutants into the air or water that other nations breathe or drink, the matter goes beyond the unitary concern of the polluting nation and becomes a matter for international negotiation. Indeed, the hydrocarbons that are emitted into the atmosphere when individual nations burn coal for generating electricity contribute to global warming and are thereby a matter of concern for the entire world.

The tensions associated with cross-border spillovers can be especially vexing when national policies generate outcomes alleged to be competitively inequitable, as in the example in which country A permits companies to emit pollutants and country B does not. Or consider a situation in which country C requires commodities, whether produced at home or abroad, to meet certain design standards, justified for safety reasons. Foreign competitors may find it too expensive to meet these standards. In that event, the standards in C act very much like tariffs or quotas, effectively narrowing or even eliminating foreign competition for domestic producers. Citing examples of this sort, producers or governments in individual nations often complain that business is not conducted on a "level playing field." Typically, the complaining nation proposes that *other* nations adjust their policies to moderate or remove the competitive inequities.

Arguments for creating a level playing field are troublesome at best. International trade occurs precisely because of differences among nations—in resource endowments, labor skills, and consumer tastes. Nations specialize in producing goods and services in which they are relatively most efficient. In a fundamental sense, cross-border trade is valuable because the playing field is *not* level.

When David Ricardo first developed the theory of comparative advantage, he focused on differences among nations owing to climate or technology. But Ricardo could as easily have ascribed the productive differences to differing "social climates" as to physical or technological climates. Taking all "climatic" differences as given, the theory of comparative advantage argues that free trade among nations will maximize global welfare.

Taken to its logical extreme, the notion of leveling the playing field implies that nations should become homogeneous in all major respects. But that recommendation is unrealistic and even pernicious. Suppose country A decides that it is too poor to afford the costs of a clean environment, and will thus permit the production of goods that pollute local air and water supplies. Or suppose it concludes that it cannot afford stringent protections for worker safety. Country A will then argue that it is inappropriate for other nations to impute to country A the value they themselves place on a clean environment and safety standards (just as it would be inappropriate to impute the A valuations to the environment of other nations). The core of the idea of political sovereignty is to permit national residents to order their lives and property in accord with their own preferences.

Which perspective about differences among nations in behind-the-border policies is more compelling? Is country A merely exercising its national preferences and appropriately exploiting its comparative advantage in goods that are dirty or dangerous to produce? Or does a legitimate international problem exist that justifies pressure from other nations urging country A to accept changes in its policies (thus

curbing its national sovereignty)? When national governments negotiate resolutions to such questions—trying to agree whether individual
nations are legitimately exercising sovereign choices or, alternatively,
engaging in behavior that is unfair or damaging to other nations—the
dialogue is invariably contentious because the resolutions depend on
the typically complex circumstances of the international spillovers
and on the relative weights accorded to the interests of particular
individuals and particular nations.

Diminished National Autonomy

As cross-border economic integration increases, governments experience greater difficulties in trying to control events within their
borders. Those difficulties, summarized by the term *diminished autonomy*, are the second set of reasons why tensions arise from the competition between political sovereignty and economic integration.

For example, nations adjust monetary and fiscal policies to influence domestic inflation and employment. In setting these policies,
smaller countries have always been somewhat constrained by foreign
economic events and policies. Today, however, all nations are constrained, often severely. More than in the past, therefore, nations may
be better able to achieve their economic goals if they work together
collaboratively in adjusting their macroeconomic policies.

Diminished autonomy and cross-border spillovers can sometimes
be allowed to persist without explicit international cooperation to
deal with them. States in the United States adopt their own tax
systems and set policies for assistance to poor single people without
any formal cooperation or limitation. Market pressures operate to
force a degree of de facto cooperation. If one state taxes corporations
too heavily, it knows business will move elsewhere. (Those familiar
with older debates about "fiscal federalism" within the United States
and other nations will recognize the similarity between those issues
and the emerging international debates about deeper integration of
national economies.) Analogously, differences among nations in regulations, standards, policies, institutions, and even social and cultural
preferences create economic incentives for a kind of arbitrage that
erodes or eliminates the differences. Such pressures involve not only
the conventional arbitrage that exploits price differentials (buying at
one point in geographic space or time and selling at another) but also

shifts in the location of production facilities and in the residence of factors of production.

In many other cases, however, cross-border spillovers, arbitrage pressures, and diminished effectiveness of national policies can produce unwanted consequences. In cases involving what economists call externalities (external economies and diseconomies), national governments may need to cooperate to promote mutual interests. For example, population growth, continued urbanization, and the more intensive exploitation of natural resources generate external diseconomies not only within but across national boundaries. External economies generated when benefits spill across national jurisdictions probably also increase in importance (for instance, the gains from basic research and from control of communicable diseases).

None of these situations is new, but technological change and the reduction of tariffs and quotas heighten their importance. When one nation produces goods (such as scientific research) or "bads" (such as pollution) that significantly affect other nations, individual governments acting sequentially and noncooperatively cannot deal effectively with the resulting issues. In the absence of explicit cooperation and political leadership, too few collective goods and too many collective bads will be supplied.

Challenges to Political Sovereignty

The pressures from cross-border economic integration sometimes even lead individuals or governments to challenge the core assumptions of national political sovereignty. Such challenges are a third source of tensions about deeper integration.

The existing world system of nation-states assumes that a nation's residents are free to follow their own values and to select their own political arrangements without interference from others. Similarly, property rights are allocated by nation. (The so-called global commons, such as outer space and the deep seabed, are the sole exceptions.) A nation is assumed to have the sovereign right to exploit its property in accordance with its own preferences and policies. Political sovereignty is thus analogous to the concept of consumer sovereignty (the presumption that the individual consumer best knows his or her own interests and should exercise them freely).

In times of war, some nations have had sovereignty wrested from them by force. In earlier eras, a handful of individuals or groups have questioned the premises of political sovereignty. With the profound increases in economic integration in recent decades, however, a larger number of individuals and groups—and occasionally even their national governments—have identified circumstances in which, it is claimed, some universal or international set of values should take precedence over the preferences or policies of particular nations.

Some groups seize on human-rights issues, for example, or what they deem to be egregiously inappropriate political arrangements in other nations. An especially prominent case occurred when citizens in many nations labeled the former apartheid policies of South Africa an affront to universal values and emphasized that the South African government was not legitimately representing the interests of a majority of South Africa's residents. Such views caused many national governments to apply economic sanctions against South Africa. Examples of value conflicts are not restricted to human rights, however. Groups focusing on environmental issues characterize tropical rain forests as the lungs of the world and the genetic repository for numerous species of plants and animals that are the heritage of all mankind. Such views lead Europeans, North Americans, or Japanese to challenge the timber-cutting policies of Brazilians and Indonesians. A recent controversy over tuna fishing with long drift nets that kill porpoises is yet another example. Environmentalists in the United States whose sensibilities were offended by the drowning of porpoises required U.S. boats at some additional expense to amend their fishing practices. The U.S. fishermen, complaining about imported tuna caught with less regard for porpoises, persuaded the U.S. government to ban such tuna imports (both direct imports from the countries in which the tuna is caught and indirect imports shipped via third countries). Mexico and Venezuela were the main countries affected by this ban; a GATT dispute panel sided with Mexico against the United States in the controversy, which further upset the U.S. environmental community.

A common feature of all such examples is the existence, real or alleged, of "psychological externalities" or "political failures." Those holding such views reject untrammeled political sovereignty for nation-states in deference to universal or non-national values. They wish to constrain the exercise of individual nations' sovereignties through international negotiations or, if necessary, by even stronger intervention.

The Management of International Convergence

In areas in which arbitrage pressures and cross-border spillovers are weak and psychological or political externalities are largely absent, national governments may encounter few problems with deeper integration. Diversity across nations may persist quite easily. But at the other extreme, arbitrage and spillovers in some areas may be so strong that they threaten to erode national diversity completely. Or psychological and political sensitivities may be asserted too powerfully to be ignored. Governments will then be confronted with serious tensions, and national policies and behaviors may eventually converge to common, worldwide patterns (for example, subject to internationally agreed norms or minimum standards). Eventual convergence across nations, if it occurs, could happen in a harmful way (national policies and practices being driven to a least common denominator with externalities ignored, in effect a "race to the bottom") or it could occur with mutually beneficial results ("survival of the fittest and the best").

Each study in this series addresses basic questions about the management of international convergence: if, when, and how national governments should intervene to try to influence the consequences of arbitrage pressures, cross-border spillovers, diminished autonomy, and the assertion of psychological or political externalities. A wide variety of responses is conceivable. We identify six, which should be regarded not as distinct categories but as ranges along a continuum.

National autonomy defines a situation at one end of the continuum in which national governments make decentralized decisions with little or no consultation and no explicit cooperation. This response represents political sovereignty at its strongest, undiluted by any international management of convergence.

Mutual recognition, like national autonomy, presumes decentralized decisions by national governments and relies on market competition to guide the process of international convergence. Mutual recognition, however, entails exchanges of information and consultations among governments to constrain the formation of national regulations and policies. As understood in discussions of economic integration within the European Community, moreover, mutual recognition entails an explicit acceptance by each member nation of the regulations, standards, and certification procedures of other members. For example, mutual recognition allows wine or liquor produced in any European Union country to be sold in all twelve member countries even if production standards in member countries differ. Doctors licensed in France are permitted to practice in Germany, and vice versa, even if licensing procedures in the two countries differ.

Governments may agree on rules that restrict their freedom to set policy or that promote gradual convergence in the structure of policy. As international consultations and monitoring of compliance with such rules become more important, this situation can be described as *monitored decentralization*. The Group of Seven finance ministers meetings, supplemented by the IMF's surveillance over exchange rate and macroeconomic policies, illustrate this approach to management.

Coordination goes further than mutual recognition and monitored decentralization in acknowledging convergence pressures. It is also more ambitious in promoting intergovernmental cooperation to deal with them. Coordination involves jointly designed mutual adjustments of national policies. In clear-cut cases of coordination, bargaining occurs and governments agree to behave differently from the ways they would have behaved without the agreement. Examples include the World Health Organization's procedures for controlling communicable diseases and the 1987 Montreal Protocol (to a 1985 framework convention) for the protection of stratospheric ozone by reducing emissions of chlorofluorocarbons.

Explicit harmonization, which requires still higher levels of intergovernmental cooperation, may require agreement on regional standards or world standards. Explicit harmonization typically entails still greater departures from decentralization in decisionmaking and still further strengthening of international institutions. The 1988 agreement among major central banks to set minimum standards for the required capital positions of commercial banks (reached through the Committee on Banking Regulations and Supervisory Practices at the Bank for International Settlements) is an example of partially harmonized regulations.

At the opposite end of the spectrum from national autonomy lies *federalist mutual governance*, which implies continuous bargaining and joint, centralized decisionmaking. To make federalist mutual governance work would require greatly strengthened supranational institutions. This end of the management spectrum, now relevant only as an analytical benchmark, is a possible outcome that can be imagined for the middle or late decades of the twenty-first century, possibly even sooner for regional groupings like the European Union.

Overview of the Brookings Project

Despite their growing importance, the issues of deeper economic integration and its competition with national political sovereignty were largely neglected in the 1980s. In 1992 the Brookings Institution initiated its project on Integrating National Economies to direct attention to these important questions.

In studying this topic, Brookings sought and received the co-operation of some of the world's leading economists, political scientists, foreign-policy specialists, and government officials, representing all regions of the world. Although some functional areas require a special focus on European, Japanese, and North American perspectives, at all junctures the goal was to include, in addition, the perspectives of developing nations and the formerly centrally planned economies.

The first phase of the project commissioned the twenty-one scholarly studies listed at the beginning of the book. One or two lead discussants, typically residents of parts of the world other than the area where the author resides, were asked to comment on each study.

Authors enjoyed substantial freedom to design their individual studies, taking due account of the overall themes and goals of the project. The guidelines for the studies requested that at least some of the analysis be carried out with a non-normative perspective. In effect, authors were asked to develop a "baseline" of what might happen in the absence of changed policies or further international cooperation. For their normative analyses, authors were asked to start with an agnostic posture that did not prejudge the net benefits or costs resulting from integration. The project organizers themselves had no presumption about whether national diversity is better or worse than international convergence or about what the individual studies should conclude regarding the desirability of increased integration. On the contrary, each author was asked to address the trade-offs in his or her issue area between diversity and convergence and to locate the area, currently and prospectively, on the spectrum of international management possibilities running between national autonomy through mutual recognition to coordination and explicit harmonization.

HENRY J. AARON   SUSAN M. COLLINS
RALPH C. BRYANT   ROBERT Z. LAWRENCE

Chapter 1

International Institutions and Economic Integration

*I*NTERNATIONAL economic space has seldom coincided perfectly with political space. The tensions arising between a world economy that is more integrated and less segmented over time and a political order that remains highly fragmented are at the core of any analysis of international economic institutions. Since 1945 those tensions have increased. Political units have proliferated after decolonization of the European empires and again with the dissolution of the Soviet Union. Norms against intervention or conquest have discouraged one age-old solution to the absence of fit between political and economic space: incorporation of additional political space within imperial or quasi-imperial frameworks. At the same time—and this trend has been marked since 1980—more governments have become attached to the value of opening to the international economy. Comprehensive programs of closure and economic nationalism have been rejected by all but a handful of states; the change has been most striking in the formerly planned economies of eastern Europe, the former Soviet Union, China, and Vietnam.

Nevertheless, states remain wary of explicit derogations from traditional notions of sovereignty and acceptance of vulnerability to the consequences of other states' policies. Because economic integration has uneven consequences for groups within particular societies, groups that may exert political influence to arrest or offset the process of integration, governments may be moved to take measures that affect the interests of other states as a result of domestic political calculus. They may also perceive national competitive advantages to be gained from modulating or managing the process of integration,

1

once again, in ways that appear to detract from the benefits enjoyed by others. Divergent national strategies became a source of international conflict when high-speed industrialization began outside the Atlantic area, in regions with very different models of political economy.

The course of integration does not run smooth. Its natural unevenness, magnified by national policies, can produce international conflict and a mix of national strategies that lowers world economic welfare. As economic integration progresses, issues of "deeper" integration emerge on the international agenda. These issues concern "behind-the-border" policies that had previously not been subjected to international scrutiny or negotiation. Indeed, whether these policies should be on the international agenda, in whole or in part, is itself a contentious issue. Instead of an older agenda of removing controls and barriers that block exchange at national perimeters, these new agenda items include conflict over domestic regulatory regimes, perceived policy spillovers, and "system friction."

The responses to this new agenda may range from agreement to disagree—relying on national policy choices—and reasserting the reality of political segmentation to centralized decisionmaking under a single political authority, conceding political autonomy entirely. In most cases, however, as described in the preface to these studies, responses involve some international agreement and oversight short of political unification: mutual recognition, coordination of policies, or explicit harmonization. These alternatives in turn have produced new international institutions and the revision of older ones to deal with the behind-the-border agenda of deeper integration. The core international economic institutions of the post-1945 era—the International Monetary Fund (IMF), the World Bank, and the General Agreement on Tariffs and Trade (GATT)—have been forced to respond to the new realities of economic integration. New regional arrangements have been negotiated in part to contend with this agenda. The portrait of an integrating world economy is one of renewed interest in international institutions and a wide variation in the design and redesign of institutions in the context of the new agenda.

Dimensions of Institutional Variation

Demonstrating the variation in international institutions that accompanies deepening economic integration is relatively easy; determining which dimensions of variation are significant is more difficult. Explaining the sources of international cooperation and investigating institutions that facilitate collective action are central to the explanation of international responses to economic integration. The investigation of institutions and regimes points to a field of mechanisms for reinforcing collaboration among governments that is broader than formal international organizations.[1] Typically, however, it is the absence or presence of institutions of any kind that has been the focus of attention. Why institutions exist at all in a presumably anarchic international setting may be an important subject when the broad sweep of international politics is considered. For the highly institutionalized international setting of the post-1945 period, however, why institutional design varies is even more important.

The dimension of institutional variation that has absorbed the attention of scholars and policymakers is that of *strength*, some measure of the effect that institutions have on the behavior of states as compared with a hypothetical environment free of such institutions. Strength is sometimes measured by compliance with international injunctions, although that measure is difficult to apply. Whether compliance or noncompliance is the typical "background condition" of international relations may be impossible to demonstrate empirically; whether particular instances of noncompliance are significant requires careful interpretation.[2] Even if the measurement of regime strength is expanded to a broader notion of influence on state behavior, the construction of difficult counterfactuals is required: is every day without an increase in bound tariffs an indicator of the strength of GATT? One reasonable proxy for strength lies in institutional design: the place awarded to monitoring and enforcement capacities suggests the significance that regime members attach to issues of compliance. A related indicator is the degree to which formal institutions dominate within the overall design: a spectrum that ranges from

1. These categories are arrayed from less formal and implicit to more formal and explicit. Regimes were defined by Krasner (1983, p. 2) as "sets of implicit or explicit principles, norms, rules, and decisionmaking procedures around which actors' expectations converge in a given area of international relations." Keohane (1988, p. 384) offered a definition of specific *institutions* as "persistent sets of rules that constrain activity, shape expectations, and prescribe roles." Given the immense amount of definitional hair-splitting that is possible, I will use *regime* and *international institution* interchangeably.

2. Chayes and Chayes (1993, pp. 177–78).

conventions or networks to formal contracts or treaties to formal organizations.[3] The relationship of formality in institutional design to behavioral outcomes may be very loose, however.

A second dimension of institutions derives from both international law and the literature on international monetary systems and policy coordination: institutions characterized by *explicit rules or injunctions* meant to inform national policies and govern the system as compared with either *episodic or institutionalized consultation or bargaining.*[4] This distinction might be characterized as one between *substantive* institutions (with rules embodying the principles of the regime) and *procedural* institutions (in which expectations of ad hoc bargaining or more regularized channels of bargaining are characteristic). This dimension has often been related to the strength of institutions—explicit and substantive rules are taken to signify stronger institutions.

Our collective image of strong international institutions has also been deeply influenced by the way in which the key postwar institutions, such as the IMF or the United Nations, were created and evolved. Bretton Woods and San Francisco were exemplars of international constitution making: cooperation was confirmed in intergovernmental formal institutions founded in contractual agreements. Institutions may also evolve over time through decentralized and incremental processes of strengthening conventions: customary international law, an "ought" that develops from "is," exemplifies the second path, as did the development of the pre-1914 gold standard. Research by Elinor Ostrom on the emergence of decentralized cooperative regimes to govern common pool resources suggests that incremental, bottom-up strategies of learning over time may produce institutions as strong as those characterized by third-party enforcement.[5] *Decentralized* creation and evolution of international institutions are typically connected to decentralized sanctioning and enforcement. Without strong evidence, *centralized* institutions with third-party enforcement mechanisms have often been associated with

3. Compare the institutional classification in Davis and others (1990) to Keohane (1989).

4. Kahler (1988); compare this to Oye's (1992) distinction between rule-governed systems and those governed by "unrestricted bargaining."

5. Ostrom's (1990) comparative research on domestic institutions has been extended to international environmental institutions. Keohane, McGinnis, and Ostrom (1993); see also Ostrom, Walker, and Gardner (1992) and Sugden (1986).

higher levels of compliance (one measure of strength). Until that presumed association can be demonstrated, the two dimensions of strength and centralization should be separated for purposes of investigation.

Two further dimensions reflect on the issue of membership in regimes. The *scope* of institutions—the degree of their differentiation according to issue-area—affects the ease of issue linkage during bargaining. Institutions that incorporate several issue-areas (both trade and money, for example) may permit the forging of constructive bargains by permitting exchanges across these issues. The scope of an institution may also reflect the influence of particular expert communities and the broader effect of cognition—a sense that certain emerging agenda items are "related" to others. *Number*—whether an institution is multilateral, plurilateral, or bilateral in membership—has often been seen to influence strongly the likelihood of forging cooperative bargains.[6] Multilateral organizations with large numbers of members may find collective action difficult as monitoring and enforcement become more difficult; decisionmaking may also become more inefficient. According to this view, plurilateral institutions with smaller membership should be able to overcome these weaknesses. Each of these presumed effects is highly dependent on institutional design, however: governance structures—voting rules, delegation, systems of representation—may offset the liabilities of large numbers.[7]

A final dimension of international institutions is their *domestic political linkages,* which may range from creation or capture by particular organized economic interests to transnational connections among particular national bureaucracies. Once again, the prevailing image of postwar international institutions has colored perceptions of the "natural" relationship between international institutions and domestic ones. An assumption that governments that serve as watchful and effective gatekeepers between their domestic constituents and

6. The category of minilateral has sometimes been equated with plurilateral; in other contexts minilateral and multilateral have been defined according to enforcement mechanism and whether coordination takes place according to generalized principles of conduct; see Yarbrough and Yarbrough (1992). Here, to avoid confusion, *bilateral, plurilateral,* and *multilateral* are used to describe institutions that coordinate the policies of two, few (or several), and many members.

7. Kahler (1993).

international institutions has survived despite developments that call into question this view of governments as both adversarial toward international institutions and protective of their constituents. First, although the central problem of cooperation among governments has dominated investigation of international institutions, much of the methodology of that investigation was borrowed from the study of institution building among private economic agents. The possibility of such private or quasi-private regimes also exists internationally. Certain intergovernmental institutions may simply "bless" contracts agreed by private actors through a process of delegation. Intergovernmental institutions or agreements may also encourage private adjustment strategies. Also, despite their image as effective gatekeepers, governments may provide direct access for nongovernmental actors to dispute settlement mechanisms or decisionmaking within international institutions. Private agents may in turn become a part of the enforcement mechanism of international institutions. In any case, the rigid division between intergovernmental institutions and both private and domestic actors deserves reconsideration.

Explanations for Institutional Variation

The range of variation among contemporary international institutions on these dimensions is great. Regional institutions, considered in chapter 3, provide only one example: the European Union, with strong centralized institutions and dense ties to national societies, coexists with regional free-trade agreements in North America and elsewhere that are far less centralized and narrower in scope. One popular explanation for both institutional variation on the dimension of strength and persistence of global institutions was proposed in the 1970s against a backdrop of anxiety over the apparent economic decline of the United States. Strength and stability in global regimes were associated with the presence of single hegemonic power. The persistence of most postwar regimes into the 1990s and the strengthening of some (such as the recent transformation of GATT into the World Trade Organization [WTO]) provided one difficulty for arguments based on hegemonic power. Historical and theoretical analyses have led to a consensus that hegemony is neither necessary nor sufficient for the creation or the persistence of strong international institutions.[8]

A second generation of research has borrowed from transactions cost economics to develop a demand-side theory of international regimes: institutions emerge and persist as solutions to particular collective action or contracting problems among states. Specifically, institutions reduce transaction costs and, perhaps most important, provide information to their members, enabling the conclusion of mutually beneficial agreements.[9] A somewhat different set of arguments suggests that international institutions assist in the evolution of cooperation under the conditions of an iterated prisoner's dilemma game by altering payoff structures, lengthening the shadow of the future, or enhancing communication.[10] In each of these cases, however, the beneficial effects of a regime in encouraging a preferred collective outcome risks providing a less-than-satisfactory functional explanation for the emergence of institutions: institutions emerge and persist because they satisfy a need or demand for the functions described (such as reduction of transaction costs). One avenue of rescue involves selection mechanisms that would sort and eliminate institutions that fail to provide these collective benefits, much as a market sorts and eliminates firms. International institutions, however, rarely die; they simply fade away (or are ignored). There may be some institutional competition at the international level, but it is weak. Another alternative is to weaken the functional logic and transform the elaboration of institutions into an instrumental problem-solving process by demonstrating that "institutions and the social practices to be explained were designed to fulfill anticipated functions."[11]

Whatever their usefulness in explaining institutional formation in a setting of self-interested states, arguments based on functions that international institutions fulfill cannot easily explain variation *among* institutions on the dimensions described earlier. Another argument similar in style to these demand-side explanations does attempt to

8. For a sampling of critical views, see Keohane (1984); Snidal (1985); Eichengreen (1989).
9. For an early statement, see Keohane (1984, pp. 85–109), also Yarbrough and Yarbrough (1992, pp. 111–33).
10. Oye (1985).
11. Keohane (1984, pp. 81–82); Yarbrough and Yarbrough (1992, pp. 126–30); Haggard and Simmons (1987).

account for such variation by presenting institutions as a response to the incentives presented in particular strategic interactions.[12] For example, "dilemmas of common interests" (games of collaboration), in which the incentives to defect are high, are associated with regimes that provide formal organizations capable of both identifying defectors and sanctioning violators. (The familiar prisoner's dilemma game is one exemplar of a game of collaboration.) Games of coordination ("dilemmas of common aversion"), in which conflict over multiple equilibria may be intense but likelihood of defection from any of those equilibria is low, are associated with less formal institutions that may provide information but serve no sanctioning role. Finally, assurance games have been described as requiring little institutional underpinning, because the incentives for opportunistic behavior are nil. Lisa Martin argued, however, that even in these instances informal institutions may assist in the assessment of actor preferences through providing information on domestic political preferences and arrangements.[13]

This style of explanation for the characteristics of institutions suffers from the shortcomings of functional logic outlined above: although, as Martin argued, "certain norms or types of formal organizations will be either dysfunctional or inefficient under specific conditions," the weak environmental selection on international institutions and the strong influence of their great-power principals may cause other domestic political logics to override the functional logic.[14] And assessing the "strategic functionalism" of a particular institutional arrangement requires an accurate reading of national preferences ex ante. Ambiguities are likely to abound. For example, harmonization of national policies is often taken as exemplary of a coordination game, but it is far from clear, when harmonization is aimed at deeply entrenched practices with strong constituencies, that the incentives to defect from the bargain reached are inconsequential. Whether a harmonized outcome represents the equilibrium of a coordination or a collaboration game is highly dependent on the domestic contexts of players.

Domestic politics, therefore, provides both a necessary supplement to these explanations that are based on the efficiency of institutions in

---

12. Martin (1993); Snidal (1985); Stein (1990, pp. 25–54).
13. Martin (1993, p. 108).
14. Martin (1993, p. 108).

particular international settings. In defining the preferences of states, domestic political variables are central. Also, domestic politics may offer alternative explanations for international institutions: self-interested politicians may seek to construct institutional solutions as a response, not only to international dilemmas of cooperation but to domestic political dilemmas as well. One model of national preferences is *interest* driven: international institutions may reflect distributional conflicts within member societies—the balance between those economic players, whether organized groups, corporations, or other agents, that have an interest in furthering economic integration or arresting its progress (or altering the terms of integration). Rational politicians, responding to those interests (mediated by particular political institutions), will supply international institutions to satisfy those interests. In extreme cases, the international institutions, like domestic ones, may be "captured" by particular groups (the European Union's Common Agricultural Policy may be an example of this phenomenon). International institutions may also provide convenient commitment devices for politicians who wish to signal their attachment to a particular policy line, such as combating inflation or liberalizing trade. The commitment link is two way: particular domestic institutional configurations may also enhance the credibility of international commitments. It may be difficult to discern in certain cases whether particular international regimes shore up the credibility of domestic commitments or national policy anchors (such as the Bundesbank or the Federal Reserve) grant credibility to those regimes.

Knowledge-based explanations highlight the role that new knowledge or changed understanding and beliefs may play in shaping the elite in international institution building. International regimes embody principles and norms as well as serving particular cooperative bargains. The sources of those institutionalized ideas may lie in the domestic milieu of particular member states or in transnational expert communities (epistemic communities), "professionals with recognized expertise and competence in a particular domain and an authoritative claim to policy-relevant knowledge within that domain or issue-area."[15] Shared understandings of international issues and likely institutional solutions serve to narrow the range of possible cooperative bargains. Because nations often have divergent prefer-

15. Haas (1992, p. 3).

ences over which institutional paths to cooperation should be followed, ideas may provide useful focal points for agreement.[16] Richard Cooper argued, for example, that only when broad scientific consensus on contagious diseases was reached in the late nineteenth century did a basis for international institutions to control the international spread of disease become possible.[17] The history of international economic institutions and their evolution has been influenced by the changing consensus of expert opinion on issues such as exchange rates (fixed versus flexible) or the applicability of GATT principles to new domains.

Teasing apart interest-based and knowledge-based explanations is difficult. The inclusion of services in the Uruguay Round and the WTO (a widening of scope) resulted from efforts to reconstruct a domestic coalition for liberalized trade in the United States, from the growing weight of services firms in the American economy, and from a much longer process of intellectual conversion that made it possible to situate services in the GATT framework. Whether interest-based or knowledge-based, however, explanations based on domestic political variables can also be used to reintroduce power into the determination of international institutional outcomes. Explanations of international institutions as responses to market failures often ignore the asymmetries in capabilities among players within particular issue-areas. The preferences of more powerful actors—whether interest- or knowledge-based—will be reflected more consistently in institutional outcomes.

Demand-side explanations for international institutions are based on the benefits that such institutions provide by reducing transaction costs or supplying information. Such accounts do not adequately explain the degree of observed institutional variation. Whether institutions are present or not may be owed in part to such perceived benefits, but any number of institutional solutions may provide those benefits. The underlying strategic setting—the particular cooperative problem that exists—may well be associated with institutions that have a particular shape on the dimensions described: clear rules and centralized enforcement, for example, when the incentives to defect are high. Arriving at an estimate of the national preferences that

16. Goldstein and Keohane (1993, pp. 17–19).
17. Cooper (1989, p. 240).

determine that underlying strategic setting, however, pushes one back to domestic political and economic variables that determine national choices. For each of these explanations, the deepening of economic integration may produce patterns that influence institutional formation and change. The relationship between economic integration and variation in institutional dimensions is discussed next.

Economic Integration and Institutional Variation

The advance of economic integration may have predictable effects on international institutions through any of the causal avenues described earlier: posing new dilemmas of collective action that require institutional evolution or innovation, altering the preferences and capabilities of states through changes in the internal alignment of interests, and creating uncertainties that require new knowledge and draw on different expert communities. One simple and powerful set of predictions has pervaded discussion of economic integration and its effects on institutional design, however: economic integration will create demand for overcoming the disadvantages of political segmentation and maximizing the gains from economic exchange by coordinating or harmonizing national policies. This demand in turn (on the logic presented earlier) will lead to the creation of stronger, more centralized, and rule-based international institutions that are wider in scope.

Parallel to such predictions but resting on a base in political economy are models in which an interest-driven process produces policy spillover, which in turn strengthens institutions and widens their scope. In some instances, institutional scope may widen to inhibit policy shifting that has adverse consequences for previous gains from exchange, preventing the substitution of one set of government policies or barriers for those that are internationally constrained (nontariff barriers for tariffs, for example). A broader set of arguments, resembling neofunctionalist models of European economic integration, holds that policies elaborated to accomplish one task are expanded (and with them the scope of international institutions) to deal with the effects of previous integrative steps. This policy upgrading implies further institutionalization.[18] A somewhat similar logic in

18. The locus classicus of this approach is Haas (1964).

favor of European monetary integration has been outlined by Jeffry Frieden: a growing number of private economic agents that are engaged in cross-border transactions (and their representatives) will press for greater predictability and stability (a lowering of risk) through a higher degree of coordination in exchange rate policies. That coordination implies the further elaboration of European institutions.[19] Whether in purely economic or more politicized form, these models of the effects of economic integration predict that integration will spawn a heightened demand for stronger rule-based institutions with greater enforcement capabilities. In other words, institutions will evolve in the direction of becoming more "statelike."

These predictions include *two* steps, each of which is subject to challenge: economic integration produces a bias toward harmonization of national policies, and integration also creates demand for stronger international institutions. The idea that economic exchange requires harmonization of an array of national policies behind the border was criticized forcefully by Harry Johnson in the early years of the European Community. Johnson argued against both the harmonization bias in much commentary on economic integration and the predictions of inevitable institutionalization in a free-trade area:

> The need for harmonization *additional to what is already required* of countries extensively engaged in world trade is relatively slight . . . such harmonization is more a matter of choosing to augment the benefits of free trade than of being required to harmonize as a result of free trade. . . . The problems of harmonization are such as can be handled by negotiation and consultation according to well-established procedures among the governments concerned, rather than such as to require elaborate international agreements.[20]

As Johnson pointed out, even if further harmonization and institutionalization seem necessary to maximize the economic gains from integration, such a calculation implies that the gains from harmonization outweigh other social objectives, because "'distortions' may be the deliberate choice of governmental policy."[21] The maximization of

19. Frieden (1993).
20. Johnson (1972, pp. 397–98).
21. Johnson (1972, p. 405); see also Robson (1987, p. 62).

economic welfare may also depend on the standard to which policies are harmonized among the national alternatives.[22]

The simple set of predictions that connects stronger international institutions with advancing economic integration provides a benchmark in exploring institutional variation under these conditions. Other explanatory approaches produce predictions that are both plausible and conflicting. The effects of economic integration on the underlying strategic interactions among governments are unclear. On the one hand, the progress of integration may produce a growing alignment of national preferences and resulting interactions among national policies so that cheating or opportunistic behavior is less of an issue. Issue density and reputational concerns in a setting of repeated interaction could make self-enforcement easier, and institutions could be informal and weaker, concentrating on information exchange. On the other hand, economic integration, by raising the issue of harmonizing national policies behind the border, could produce new dilemmas of monitoring and enforcement because of the number of entrenched domestic interests involved. Because issues of this kind are often opaque and are intimately related to the core of domestic political competence, cheating may become more likely rather than less likely, in part because the observation of national policies is more difficult.

Interest-based domestic political explanations provide an even more fundamental challenge to a simple association of economic integration with stronger international institutions. Rather than assuming that those interests favoring increased integration will dominate domestic political choices over time, an interest-driven approach emphasizes the distributional conflict that surrounds integration and the competing strategies advanced by those interests that favor integration and those that are disadvantaged by it (or perceive themselves to be). The relative weight of those interests across states will produce different choices on the international strategy to be pursued (for example, national autonomy rather than harmonization) and on the institutions that will be coupled to that strategy. For example, although pro-integration interests are typically seen as favoring harmonization and institutional elaboration to oversee such harmonization, those interests may, in some circumstances, prefer national policy convergence forced by economic means rather than international

22. On harmonization of technical standards, see Hansson (1990, p. 85).

pressure or agreement. In some cases, those disadvantaged by integration may propose autonomous national policies to protect their interests; in other cases, harmonization confirmed by international agreement may seem the best alternative to competitive convergence of national policies.

Institutional design, therefore, may reflect both political dynamics in uneasy amalgam. The North American Free Trade Agreement (NAFTA), for example, contained provisions that aimed at removing some behind-the-border restrictions on trade and investment (promoted by pro-integration forces) and other provisions (the environmental and labor-side agreements) that effectively sought upward harmonization of domestic standards by groups anxious over the effects of further integration. An analysis of this kind first requires an assessment of the strategies forwarded by interests that perceive themselves affected by economic integration *within* nations and then the outcome achieved *between* nations through international bargaining. The mere presence of international institutions or their "strengthening" may reflect a more complex political dynamic than the simple advance of integration and its supporters. The complexity is increased by filtering of interest definition by changing knowledge (or interpretation) of the gains to be made (or the losses risked) by particular strategies. To return to the NAFTA example, the scale of prospective gains and losses for particular American interests was the subject of hot domestic political debate (and was probably overestimated by both sides). Future scenarios and their underlying assumptions, whatever their qualities as scientific analysis, both shaped and were shaped by political discourse on NAFTA.

The predictions that can be drawn from this politically driven model are complex when compared to the close association between stronger institutions and economic integration that is drawn in the simple economic model described earlier. Specific hypotheses regarding national policies or international institutional outcomes require first weighting the preferences of groups internally given their influence on national policy and then weighting national capabilities and influence within a particular issue-area. Consider, for example, the preferences of organized groups toward national policies and their harmonization under conditions of deeper economic integration. As an approximation, those groups that perceive themselves as losing from economic integration would probably prefer policies of national autonomy (permitting restraints on further integration), with harmonization to national standards as a second-best outcome (serving to protect their constituents from policy competition). The beneficiaries of economic integration (for example, internationally oriented firms) would probably prefer international harmonization to national standards as a preferred outcome (in those policy areas that affect their cross-border transactions) and coordination of national policies or harmonization to an agreed international standard as a second-best outcome. National autonomy that permitted restrictions—at the border or behind the border—on further integration would be the worst outcome from the point of view of these interests.

If this ordering of preferences is roughly accurate, then "harmonization" could become the basis of national policies in the face of economic integration, although harmonization would typically mean harmonization of very different behind-the-border policies. Harmonization in this case would not be the result of a careful consideration of the economic gains to be made from harmonizing national policies but would instead be the result of domestic political equilibrium. If the balance of influence domestically were shifted in one direction or another (toward pro-integration or anti-integration forces), then the international stance of the government in question would change as well.

Internationally, substantial asymmetries in bargaining power could be predicted to result in harmonization to the more powerful partner's own standards. In bargaining situations and issue-areas in which national capabilities are more evenly balanced, mutually agreed harmonization or negotiated mutual recognition of national standards is more likely. Mutual recognition could provide a stable international equilibrium (backed by a balance of domestic political forces) that requires less institutionalization than predicted by models that foresee inevitable widening and strengthening of institutions in the face of integration.

In assessing the likelihood of rule-governed institutions or more ad hoc arrangements of consultation or bargaining, the model based on functional demands driven by economic integration points toward the likelihood of rule-governed structures. Such institutions are likely to lower transaction costs more; private agents engaged in cross-border transactions will demand the transparency and predictability embodied in rule-based policy regimes. However, a prediction based more on domestic interests and knowledge could predict that rule-based institutions will prove fragile in the face of an agenda of behind-the-border issues based on conflicting policy regimes and psychological externalities (in environmental policy, for example). Forging rule-governed institutions capable of dealing with the myriad "distortions" and "barriers" that can be alleged by international competitors may be impossible. Such a portrait suggests higher demand for arrangements centered on procedures triggering negotiations, consultations, and mediation of disputes rather than substantive rules.

Although most of the institutions considered in this study are formal and relatively well established, further institutional innovation and evolution may occur through either constitutional revision and formal contracting carried out "top down" or decentralized agreements in which new rules and norms emerge "bottom up." One plausible hypothesis is that economic integration will affect institutional design on this dimension in a curvilinear fashion. Decentralized institutions and institutional change are most likely in two circumstances. First, when economic integration is shallow and information about national preferences is scarce and expensive, a substantial degree of information-gathering is required before stronger and more centralized institutions can emerge. Second, decentralization can re-emerge at the other end of this arc of information, when information about the preferences and reputations of international partners is plentiful and cheap. Under these circumstances, decentralized reputation-based systems may again be sufficient. Decentralization may serve different purposes in these two situations then: an initial information search and confidence-building role and an efficient institutional solution among partners operating in an information-rich environment. Centralized institutions with greater monitoring and enforcement capabilities might be expected in intermediate situations, when transparency has increased but uncertainty remains regarding the preferences of governments.

The conventional prediction that the scope of international institutions will necessarily widen with economic integration can be set beside two alternative predictions, based on bargaining power and on knowledge. Scope may be highly dependent on perceived bargaining advantages through cross-issue linkage. Institutional scope will be widened when an actor or set of actors perceives benefits from linking two previously unconnected issues. An alternative explanation for institutional scope centers on uncertainty and expert knowledge. Given the uncertainties that surround many of the causal connections in the process of economic integration (for example, links between investment and trade or environmental spillovers and trade), the incorporation of new issue-areas into existing institutions may be knowledge driven: scope will be widened when causal connections are documented by authoritative expert communities.

The effects of economic integration appear particularly indeterminate in changing the balance among large-number (multilateral), plurilateral, and bilateral institutions. Decisionmaking efficiency and the unevenness of the processes of integration itself argue for greater numbers of smaller-number institutions. The history of international institutions since 1945 demonstrates a record of great-power plurilateralism, even when embedded in regimes of large membership. The agenda produced by intensified economic integration will only surface among particular groups of states, often although not always geographically proximate. However, as larger numbers of economies are brought into the global capitalist order (as they have been for the past decade), free riding by those outside the rules of established institutions has become less acceptable to the most powerful members. Their concern over costly free riding predicts greater reliance on global institutions that will constrain the larger number of governments engaged in the international economy. The tension between these two dynamics has probably intensified as economic integration has extended beyond the Atlantic area. One predicted resolution is the proliferation of both "multispeed" organizations and plurilateral agreements among the "like-minded" as favored alternatives.

As economic integration produces a new agenda of policy spillovers and behind-the-border obstacles to exchange, the linkages between international institutions and the domestic politics of their members become particularly important. One possible outcome concerns monitoring and enforcement of international agreements: given the difficulties that states may have in monitoring compliance when behind-the-border issues are at stake, international institutions involved in monitoring may incorporate direct participation by private agents. A second possibility is that private actors may forge their own bargains to govern coordination and adjustment as economic integration progresses: the demand for international institutions under such circumstances may actually decline, or the institutions themselves may simply preside over fundamentally private (nongovernmental) bargains.

Taken together these hypotheses about the effects of economic integration on international institutions provide a test of the parsimonious economic model—that integration produces stronger institutions that are more centralized, rule based, and wider in scope—with its chief contenders, whether those emphasizing the strategic interactions among states or the interest- and knowledge-based explanations of institutional design that are grounded in domestic political dynamics. If the institutions emerging in response to the agenda of deeper economic integration appear to vary in ways that are not directly related to the level of integration, then the rival hypotheses may appear more plausible. Given the limited number of institutional observations and the lags that may elapse between advancing integration, political demands responding to that integration, and institutional outcomes that result from those demands, this study can be no more than a preliminary test of the plausibility of some of these hypotheses.

Three Conventional Views of International Institutions

This preliminary test of the effects of economic integration on the design and evolution of international institutions must guard against certain intellectual predispositions that have colored investigations of international governance. Political scientists, lawyers, and economists have contributed to the renewed burst of research on institutions; each discipline has brought to that study its own prejudices and assumptions. Political scientists have focused on the questions set by neorealist skeptics: why and how states cooperate. Despite occasional disclaimers, successful interstate cooperation is often seen as an unmitigated good, a view vigorously criticized by those who see much intergovernmental cooperation as a self-protective cartel that may exploit the citizens of member states and those societies that stand outside the collusive bargain. Political scientists have also tended to embrace naive institutionalism, a belief that more institutionalization (as measured on the dimensions described above) is likely to be the most efficacious means of confirming cooperative bargains.[23]

23. The phrase *naive institutionalism* was coined by Robert O. Keohane in his comments on this study.

Many lawyers share a predictable preference for rule-based institutions that have strong means for adjudicating disputes. John H. Jackson argued that evolution from a "power-oriented approach" to a "rule-oriented approach" (which he labels as describing the arc of civilization) "must occur in international affairs, and . . . as to international economic affairs particularly, there are strong arguments for pursuing evenhandedly, and with a fixed direction, progress in international procedures toward a rule-oriented approach."[24] John Barton, however, noted an American (one might add, American legal) predilection for the contractual or constitution-building approach to international institutions as compared to a more "organic" model of institutional development.[25] This legalism has strongly influenced our views of which institutions are more likely to be successful and has even colored our definition of success.

Economists have approached international institutions bearing a belief in economic functionalism—that underlying economic processes will produce institutions of a particular kind—and, as Harry Johnson noted, an implicit normative bias toward expanding global economic welfare and maximizing the gains from economic integration (while setting aside other political or social goals).[26] That these beliefs have produced a bias toward centralized and formal institutions is more puzzling, because the new institutional economics, which has inspired so much research on institutional variation, has also explicitly turned its attention toward the costs and limits of "legal centralism" and "discretionary centralized authority." One of the key lessons of the new institutional economics is to be "permissive of private ordering."[27] This new analysis of institutions points toward a far more careful weighing of the costs and benefits of particular institutional forms.

Together, these three disciplinary perspectives—political, legal, and economic—have too often pushed the investigation and evaluation of international institutions toward a "European" model of the future: intensified economic integration implies stronger, more formal institutions that become wider and wider in scope. Institu-

24. Jackson (1984, pp. 1571–72).
25. Barton (1984).
26. See Johnson (1972, p. 405).
27. For a recent statement by Oliver Williamson, see Williamson (1994, p. 11); also Williamson (1985, pp. 20–21, 164–66); Milgrom and Roberts (1990, pp. 79–81).

tions become more effective as they become more "statelike." One additional benefit of this review of the variety of institutional responses to economic integration may be to question this model of institutional evolution and desirable institutional design under new economic circumstances. What we may discover are multiple devices, emerging in a process of trial-and-error learning, that permit politicians and publics to share the benefits of economic integration and maintain a valued degree of autonomy for the future.

In the chapters that follow, the response of global institutions to economic integration is considered first: GATT, which has evolved from a centerpiece of shallow integration, dealing with a limited number of at-the-border barriers, to the favored global locus for managing many of the recent conflicts arising from economic integration, and the IMF, which saw its role in managing the exchange-rate system eroded, in part because of global financial integration and in part because of the unwillingness of its principals to subordinate macroeconomic policy coordination to stringent international surveillance. Together with the World Bank, it has regained some of its former position, first as a convenient focal point for managing the debt crisis and its threat to the financial system, and, more significantly, as a means of ensuring structural adjustment (policy adjustments) in developing and ex-socialist economies. After accounting for the evolution of these two institutions, I turn to global regulatory regimes and their transformation under conditions of heightened economic integration: two of these are sectoral (telecommunications and financial regulation) and the third deals with international environmental issues.

Chapter 3 considers the array of regional institutions that have appeared or enjoyed a revival in the 1990s. The greater capacities of regional institutions to deal with many of the issues arising from economic integration provide one explanation for this resurgence. Their variation on the institutional dimensions given earlier is immense: from the nascent institutions of the Asia-Pacific region to the recent free-trade agreements between Australia and New Zealand and among the North American economies to the European Union, which itself displays hesitations and indecisions about its institutional future.

The final chapter summarizes the pattern of institutional variation, global and regional. The preliminary hypotheses and predictions presented in this introduction are evaluated, and tentative conclusions are presented on the efficacy and likely success of the institutional solutions that have emerged in response to a changing international economic and political environment.

Chapter 2

Global Institutions and Deeper Integration

THE General Agreement on Tariffs and Trade (GATT) and the International Monetary Fund (IMF) have been core global institutions in the management of shallow integration—integration based on the removal of barriers to exchange at the border and limited coordination of national policies—since World War II. In an era when financial liberalization has heightened global financial integration and behind-the-border policy conflicts are more prominent, their fortunes have been mixed and their institutional trajectories divergent, as they have been from the start. Although GATT had been the target of vehement complaints from critics who argued that it was incapable of dealing with the variegated issues of system friction, the institution emerged from the Uruguay Round with broader scope and a strengthened institutional design. Despite its central role in managing the systemic threats of the debt crisis and inducing policy change in both developing and ex-socialist economies, the IMF has played a marginal role in the management of policy spillovers among the industrialized countries since the breakdown of the regime of fixed exchange rates two decades ago.

Despite their mixed fortunes in the era of deeper integration, both organizations have attracted larger numbers of members, approaching universal status in their membership.[1] In this chapter, the re-

1. Arthur Dunkel, then director-general of GATT, noted in March 1993 that fifteen countries had joined GATT since the beginning of the Uruguay Round in 1986; twelve more were negotiating accession, and twenty-five others had either obtained or requested observer status, typically the first step before accession.

sponses of these two global institutions and the broader regimes in which they are embedded to the issues and conflicts posed by advancing economic integration are examined. The strengths and weaknesses of their institutional characteristics are compared in the new environment. In a final section of the chapter, the management of three global regulatory regimes—financial markets, telecommunications, and the environment—and their relationship to the global regimes (particularly GATT) are compared. They represent alternative paths through which the issues of deeper integration (and wider integration) are governed internationally.

GATT: Institutional Evolution and Trade Liberalization

Arguments over the institutional dimensions of GATT have persisted since its founding, in part because it was not the institution planned to manage multilateral trade relations after World War II. When the United States failed to ratify the Havana Charter establishing the International Trade Organization (ITO)—a formal centralized partner to the IMF—GATT, a framework for negotiating multilateral trade agreements, became the only global organization governing trade relations. For those who equated strength with formal rule-based organizations, this flawed birth continued to mark GATT, weakening the trade regime and leaving it prey to "power-oriented" rather than "rules-oriented" diplomacy. Improving GATT performance required constitutional revision and institutional strengthening. An equally powerful view, however, if not among scholars then among diplomats and policymakers, holds that the flexibility and openness of the GATT framework enhance its usefulness as an instrument in the resolution of international trade disputes.[2]

In the absence of the ITO, GATT took shape as a combination of multilateral tariff agreements plus substantive obligations concerning the conduct of national trade policy. From the start, it was not defined as an organization, which seemed at first to place limits on its institutionalization. GATT rules or injunctions were typically qualified, often in GATT itself or in the practices that evolved in the postwar

2. Jackson (1992, pp. 85–88).

trade regime.[3] From the start, the Protocol of Provisional Application "grandfathered" several domestic measures that violated the substantive obligations of GATT (contained in part II of the General Agreement).[4] GATT obligations dealing with border barriers to trade and embodying the norm of liberalization were undoubtedly the clearest: contracting parties undertook not to raise negotiated (bound) tariff levels and to remove quotas (quantitative restrictions). Even the latter prohibition permitted exceptions for developing countries and for balance of payments reasons. Liberalization was implemented through negotiations embodying the principle of reciprocity—not formally mentioned in GATT, although negative reciprocity (tit-for-tat retaliation for violations of obligations) was restrained by GATT oversight. And liberalization itself was qualified by safeguard provisions (particularly article XIX) to protect domestic interests that experience "serious injury" from liberalization, although those provisions also included an obligation to consult.

Two other obligations—nondiscrimination (article I) and national treatment (article III)—were central to GATT. The unconditional most favored nation (MFN) obligation (nondiscrimination) was circumscribed by GATT's article XXIV, permitting customs unions and free-trade areas that met GATT criteria of liberalization, transparency, and coverage. Developing countries were later granted "special and differential" treatment under GATT; an entirely new class of members was granted positive discrimination, a gift whose wisdom was widely questioned.[5] National treatment—a GATT obligation not to discriminate between foreign and domestic products—was restricted in scope to goods. The injunction did not apply to services or to investment: granting right of establishment was not a GATT obligation.

The structure of GATT injunctions clearly reflected the domestic political sensitivity of trade policy measures: national governments (and rational politicians) were not willing to concede discretion over tariffs and quotas without the possibility of offering political rewards (reciprocity) or offsetting political pain (safeguards). The same wari-

3. On the norms and rules of the GATT regime, see Finlayson and Zacher (1981); Jackson (1992, pp. 39–44).

4. Jackson (1992, pp. 34–37).

5. For a skeptical view, see Hudec (1987).

ness regarding sovereignty characterized the strengthening of the regime over time. Strength, it will be recalled, could be measured in several ways. On one of those measures, the formal character of the institutions, GATT from the outset appeared weak: collective decisions are taken by the "Contracting Parties acting jointly." A second measure of strength is that of compliance with institutional rules. Using this criterion, different observers diverge in their judgments of the trade regime. For some, in part because of its narrow scope and its ambiguous injunctions, GATT could not underpin a trade regime that would seriously influence national behavior; the loopholes were simply too large. For others, using an implicit benchmark of earlier historical periods and noting that GATT presided over an era of unparalleled consensual trade liberalization, compliance with the spirit, if not the letter, of GATT is viewed more positively.

Perhaps the most precise efforts to assess the strength of GATT have been directed at the dispute settlement mechanism (DSM). Characteristically, articles XXII and XXIII of GATT, on which the later development of dispute settlement was based, do not mention the term. The gradual accretion of practices under this label was only codified at the time of the Tokyo Round in the 1979 Understanding on Dispute Settlement.[6] As it evolved before the Uruguay Round, GATT dispute settlement was based on a decentralized model: GATT itself could only facilitate enforcement of agreements; it possessed no enforcement power itself. Without a complaint from a contracting party (on the grounds of "nullification or impairment" of the benefits under GATT), the dispute settlement process could not be set in motion. The entire process was an unusual (in the context of international economic institutions) mixture of consultation, negotiation, and mediation, in which only the middle stage (the use of a panel of experts) displayed some "impartial and judicial elements."[7] Even so, the panel reports remained a "legal patchwork," "persuasive, not decisive documents" in the eyes of some lawyers.[8] After the panel forwards its report and if efforts at negotiated settlement fail, the contracting parties can authorize retaliation by the complaining party

6. Assessments of the dispute settlement mechanism are given in Castel (1989, pp. 835–43); Price (1992); Hudec, Kennedy, and Sgarbossa (1993); Jackson (1992, pp. 98–100); Mora (1993); Hilf (1990).

7. Hilf (1990, p. 73).

8. Pescatore (1993, p. 13).

(although such an authorization has only been given once in the history of GATT).[9]

This mix of negotiation and quasi adjudication in the process of dispute settlement could be seen as either a shortcoming or a strength. Other weaknesses were more apparent. Consensus decisionmaking in GATT permitted the party complained against to halt the proceedings at nearly any stage. In the eyes of some, the DSMs were also underused, given the number of trade disputes in the international arena.[10] However, compared to the large number of conciliation and DSMs in other agreements (procedures that were often neglected), the GATT record of use does not appear low. The use of the DSM has also demonstrated considerable fluctuation over time: increasing during the early years, dropping precipitously during the 1960s, and then increasing again during the 1980s. Coupled with increased use over the past decade, however, was a marked increase in noncompliance with panel reports on the part of the European Community and particularly the United States.[11] Throughout the history of GATT, use of the DSM has been concentrated on the "great powers"; relatively few complaints have been lodged by developing countries or by smaller contracting parties, perhaps because the risk of retaliation by a large trading power (in trade policy or in other issue-areas) appears too great or because the ultimate threat of retaliation by a small trader against a large trader is not likely to be effectual.

Despite an increase in the use of the GATT DSM in the 1980s, it is not clear what statistical measures of this kind signify about the GATT regime. First, the dispute settlement process is only the tip of an iceberg of trade disputes; the growth of disputes "settled" on a bilateral basis outside GATT may be an equally important measure of strength in the trade regime. The existence of a GATT DSM and the threat of its use may well have influenced the settlement of conflicts that are not brought to GATT: the threat of a "court action" may often induce a negotiated settlement in domestic law. This standard of judgment raises any estimate of the strength of GATT. Perhaps the

9. The case involved seven years in which the Netherlands was authorized to suspend concessions against U.S. imports; it did not carry out the suspension, and American behavior did not change.

10. In forty-two years, only 207 complaints were filed; see Hudec, Kennedy, and Sgarbossa (1993, p. 3).

11. Hudec, Kennedy, and Sgarbossa (1993, p. 98).

most accurate measure would be a difficult counterfactual one: how many trade conflicts are resolved (within GATT or outside it) that would, in the absence of the DSM and GATT, persist or grow in intensity, perhaps ending in trade wars? In similar fashion, the enforcement powers of GATT may be given far too much attention. The real force of GATT injunctions and panel findings may be the threat that GATT "will unravel if a sufficient number of countries circumvent its rules and procedures."[12] Finally, an important issue is raised for legalists who argued for clearer rules and more certain enforcement in GATT and the future World Trade Organization (WTO): would the DSM have been used to the degree that it has (particularly by the large trading members) without the important, if debilitating, escape hatch of consensus decisionmaking? A rule-based system that presses toward treating its members with complete equality could find that its most powerful members, whose trade conflicts could endanger the entire multilateral system, avoid using this means of resolving their disputes.

The record of use and compliance in the DSM is only one measure, and an ambiguous one, of changes in the strength of GATT institutions. GATT has evolved toward a more formal and well-defined institutional character. The absence of a "constitution," so alarming to the legalist view, has not prevented considerable institutional innovation. The General Agreement created no institutional structure, except for an executive secretary. The elaboration of the present institutions—a director-general, a secretariat, the GATT Council (enhancing decisionmaking efficiency), and the DSM described above—took place over time as the result of "practice and need, rather than on any institutional grand design."[13] Such institutional flexibility was particularly important, because the General Agreement was very difficult to amend, a principal explanation for the gradual proliferation of side agreements. Despite its useful adaptability in response to the changing agendas of its members, GATT before the Uruguay Round of trade negotiations remained "a compact that establishes communication and conventions to facilitate coordination" of national policies.[14] With the exception of limited monitoring

---

12. Hoekman (1993, p. 50).
13. Winham (1992, p. 66).
14. Richardson (1988, p. 172).

capabilities, GATT did not become an institution with independent delegated enforcement power.

On other institutional dimensions, GATT also evolved. Although GATT is a multilateral institution with a relatively large number of contracting parties, its style of governance has typically been pluri-lateral. Early on and particularly from the 1960s, the core of decision-making and the pattern of trade negotiation was dominated by bargains among the major trading powers: the United States, the European Community, and Japan. As Winham argued, "What was a multilateral negotiation in name became a large, complicated series of bilateral (or plurilateral) negotiations in fact."[15] Although GATT was the center of the global trade regime, the scope of its trade liberaliza-tion efforts was limited primarily to trade in manufactured goods. Agricultural trade and trade-related agricultural policies remained largely outside the GATT regime. Some categories of manufactures (textiles and apparel) were incorporated in managed trade regimes embedded loosely in the GATT framework.

Finally, GATT was characterized by very weak linkage to the domestic politics of the contracting parties. As Ostry pointed out, GATT has always lacked a continuing relationship with business, in contrast to the Business and Industry Advisory Committee of the Organization for Economic Cooperation and Development (OECD) or the close ties between financial institutions and the central banks that coordinate financial regulation. Undoubtedly, GATT enjoys a constituency among export interests in the major trading countries, but the contracting parties have not seen fit to encourage direct links between the private sector and GATT (although their trade policy processes often include private sector representation and consulta-tion).[16] A second critical link to the domestic regimes of its members has been shaped by GATT's institutional form: the ambiguous con-nection of GATT panel decisions and GATT obligations to national law. In part this link depends on domestic legal systems, which determine whether international agreements are incorporated into domestic law automatically or whether additional legislation is required. In part the uncertain legal standing of GATT itself under the Protocol of Provisional Application has influenced the status of

15. Winham (1986, p. 65).
16. Ostry (1990, pp. 3–4).

GATT within national legal systems. Although the links between international institutions and the domestic legal system do not affect the international obligations represented by GATT or other international agreements, they may have considerable import for compliance through the realignment of domestic institutions with international commitments.[17] In the major trading countries, GATT does not have the same strong connection to domestic law that, for example, the European Union (EU) treaties have within the legal systems of EU members.

Uruguay Round Agenda and the Evolution of GATT Institutions

In the first decades of GATT, liberalization efforts in successive negotiating rounds concentrated on conventional border barriers to trade: tariffs and quotas. GATT embodied a limited view of trade policy and a very spare model of integration based on removal of barriers at the border. Trade in this view is based on national differences; trade regimes in turn should devolve their institutional "work" at the lowest possible level (the principle of subsidiarity) and respect the diversity of national institutions.[18] The early GATT regime exemplified this type of limited cooperation: it aimed to remove government intrusions of a particular sort (tariffs and quantitative restrictions) on behalf of private economic agents and undistorted market signals. The set of national policies that was labeled *trade* and was of concern to GATT was a relatively short list.

Some governments preferred to maintain this careful division between external commercial policies, subject to the scrutiny of other contracting parties, and domestic arrangements that remain the prerogative of sovereign states and their constituents. GATT's own principles, however, particularly national treatment, pushed it in the direction of closer examination of internal policies that might represent new varieties of protectionism that became evident as tariffs and quotas were reduced. At the same time, articles XX and XXI of

17. For a good summary of these issues, see Jackson (1990, pp. 30–35).
18. Price (1989, pp. 24–26).

GATT qualified GATT obligations (including national treatment) in the interests of social goals that ranged from national security and "conserving natural resources" to the "protection of human, animal or plant life or health." Measures taken in pursuit of these justified goals softened GATT obligations without entirely removing them; departures from strict nondiscrimination and national treatment are permitted only to the extent necessary to achieve the stipulated goal. "Arbitrary and unjustifiable discrimination" or regulation that is a "disguised restriction on international trade" is forbidden.[19] Distinguishing between such legitimate intervention and carefully disguised protectionism would become more difficult as governments intervened to implement a wide range of social and environmental policies.

The first venture of GATT in the direction of dealing with national policy differences that affected trade occurred during the Tokyo Round when codes to reduce certain nontariff barriers to trade were negotiated. Six of the codes were rule oriented (antidumping, subsidies, standards, government procurement, customs valuation, and import licensing procedures); three were sectoral (civil aircraft, dairy products, and bovine meat). Although some of these issues were already included in GATT, at least in part, and most were closely linked to trade barriers at the border, they indicated a growing concern, particularly in the United States, over the competitive disadvantages posed by the domestic policy regimes of its trading partners. Apart from widening the scope of GATT, the codes also deviated from the norm of unconditional MFN: the United States decided to extend the benefits of three codes only to other signatories. The codes also were governed by their signatories and typically had their own DSMs, producing fears of further fragmentation in the GATT order. In most instances, evaluation of the codes after a decade is positive: exchange of information and transparency has been high. The principal exception is the subsidies code. Its dispute settlement procedures have not worked; however, the underlying problem is substantive disagreement over the interpretation of the code itself. Also, even the non-MFN codes have attracted few signatories beyond the industrialized countries—the same pattern observed in use of the DSM.[20]

19. Jackson (1992, p. 207).
20. Hoekman and Stern (1993, pp. 81–85).

Origins of the Uruguay Round: Behind-the-Border Issues and GATT

GATT's modest efforts to deal with issues of deeper integration in the Tokyo Round appeared inadequate by the 1980s. Pressure for a new trade round focused on both widening the scope of GATT to deal with behind-the-border issues of deeper integration and strengthening the institutions of the trade regime. As an agenda for a new round of trade negotiations took shape, the existing tentative approach of GATT to domestic policy regimes was broadened once again.

Three features of the new trade environment spurred the development of a new agenda for trade negotiations and arguments for broadening the scope of GATT. Two were knowledge driven: a growing awareness of the importance of the links between trade and investment in global production networks and the development of strategic trade theory. A third was interest driven: the growing unilateralism in U.S. trade policy as it fixed on the new issues of "unfair" trade. Trade and investment, which had been considered as substitutes, were increasingly viewed as complementary parts of national and corporate export strategies. The anxiety of the United States and Japan over the European Community's single-market initiative centered on investment-related issues. Criticism of Japan's "closed" market for manufactured goods centered less on government barriers to trade than on informal and opaque restrictions that curbed both imports and inward foreign investment and created a persistent asymmetry between Japan and other industrialized countries.[21] Many developing country governments deployed an array of investment incentives to shape the trade performance of investing firms, distorting trade patterns and irritating foreign investors. Ironically, as those governments liberalized their trade and investment regimes in the 1980s, such policies became more visible and more objectionable to competing governments. Such "trade-related" investment measures would become part of the Uruguay Round of trade negotiations, but they symbolized a larger agenda centered on investment and the issue of market access that investment had come to represent.

---

21. On the concerns over European investment rules, see Hufbauer (1990, pp. 39–40); Flamm (1990, pp. 271–88). On inward investment and the link to trade in Japan, see Encarnation (1992).

A second impetus to the new agenda derived from changes in trade theory that altered views of government policies designed to shape the terms of international competition in particular industries. By relaxing the assumptions of perfect competition and constant returns, strategic trade theory suggested conditions under which a government might beneficially protect or subsidize its firms. Few proponents of the new trade theory endorsed protectionism, but the new theoretical turn appeared to demote free trade from an automatic optimum to a reasonable rule of thumb.[22] Even new trade theorists who pressed the case for liberalized trade, however, argued that the new approach made behind-the-border domestic policies restricting competition or entry far more central. The line between border barriers that may legitimately be scrutinized and behind-the-border barriers excluded from "commercial policy" is further blurred.[23] The implications for international institutions such as GATT were twofold. If strategic trade interventions by governments produced tit-for-tat retaliation, the welfare of all would be reduced and national advantages could be erased. Therefore, multilateral restraint of national industrial policies through GATT or another international institution was one policy prescription that could be derived from strategic trade theory. A second implication was the need for international surveillance mechanisms, given the increased monitoring costs in tracking such "inherently opaque" government policies.[24] Both of these roles—surveillance and restraint of national policies—could potentially be filled by a broadened and strengthened GATT.

Perhaps the most significant source of pressure for a new trade round with an expanded scope was the United States. American trade policy and politics in the 1980s contributed in two ways to the opening of a new round of trade negotiations that would include issues and sectors previously excluded from GATT. The United States had long felt disadvantaged by the narrow scope of GATT. Sectors in which the United States was internationally competitive, such as agriculture and services, were not subject to GATT disciplines. A broader GATT agenda would open markets of prospective importance to American firms and rebuild a domestic political coali-

22. Krugman (1987).
23. See, for example, Richardson (1993, pp. 102–03).
24. Richardson (1988, p. 185).

tion in support of a liberalized trade and investment order. Successive United States administrations had also argued, since the negotiation of codes covering nontariff barriers in the Tokyo Round, that its exporters and investors contended with competing political economies that were organized to discriminate against outsiders. Long-standing conflicts over subsidies with Canada, the European Community, and Japan exemplified the deep divide that existed between the United States and its major trading partners on the appropriate role of government in the economy and the possible distortions that apparently "domestic" policies could add to trade relations.

The second and more immediate contribution of the United States to a new GATT round with broader scope was its increasing turn to "aggressive unilateralism." The shift in American commercial policy during the 1980s toward targeting "unfair" trading practices was in part a simple response to protectionist pressures produced by an overvalued dollar.[25] Sharp cuts in trade adjustment assistance and a distaste for overt protectionism made manipulation of the details of trade legislation—in particular, granting easier access to firms—the simplest way for a rational politician to grant relief from import competition.[26] A declining dollar did not reduce the new political dependency on these instruments, whether antidumping, countervailing duties directed against subsidies, or action against unfair trading practices. This newest turn in American trade policy exerted its own influence on the launching of the Uruguay Round. Both industrialized and developing countries sought to restrain American use of these instruments and to guarantee access to the American market. Also, the United States found that its competitors could easily mimic its policies: trading partners turned to their own versions of these instruments in classic tit-for-tat fashion. One route for restraint was regional free-trade agreements; another was negotiation under GATT. Curbs on the use of antidumping and countervailing measures—which claimed to target behind-the-border "unfairness"—became yet another item on the new GATT agenda.

25. Nivola documented the overwhelming number of trade cases in the 1980s that involved claims of both injury and "unfair" trading practices; see Nivola (1993, pp. 21, 25; table 2.2, p. 24).
26. Nivola (1993, p. 91).

Uruguay Round: Institutional Design for Deeper Integration

Incorporating new behind-the-border issues in international negotiations need not have meant a new round of negotiations under GATT or changes in that institution to address the new agenda. Many were skeptical that GATT, which had moved so hesitantly on the new agenda, could deal effectively with these issues. Throughout the Uruguay Round of negotiations, which began in September 1986 and concluded in December 1993, the eventual success of a strategy of situating these issues in GATT rather than in regional or bilateral negotiations was open to doubt. The signing of the Final Act of the Uruguay Round and the Agreement Establishing the WTO at Marrakesh in April 1994 suggested that institutional characteristics of GATT had permitted this unprecedented widening of scope and strengthening of the core trade institutions.

The Uruguay Round and its efforts to deal with the agenda of deeper integration were complicated from the start by the issue of number: a much wider participation on the part of smaller trading powers and the developing countries. The Tokyo Round had been characterized by crucial bargains struck among the United States, the European Community, and Japan (occasionally joined by Canada) and then extended to other members of GATT. The final weeks of the Uruguay Round demonstrated the continuing clout of the United States and the EU: no final agreement was possible without their assent. Nevertheless, a new and significant attachment to policies of economic opening and outward orientation among developing countries mobilized them for engagement in the Uruguay Round. Their success, actual and prospective, as traders made itself felt in the negotiations: the United States and the other industrialized countries were no longer willing to accept free riding by the developing countries on crucial bargains. Some issues—such as extension of GATT in the area of intellectual property rights—required the inclusion of developing countries to guarantee effectiveness. Any effort to strengthen GATT as an institution would also require assent by a broad coalition within the institution. Decisionmaking by consensus within GATT only strengthened the bargaining power of the developing countries.

The developing countries, however, were far less enthusiastic about the new agenda of services, intellectual property rights, and trade-related investment measures (TRIMs) than they were about institutional reform. Many could not see a positive economic gain in bringing these sectors under the GATT umbrella; others strenuously resisted encroachments on sensitive areas of national regulation. Although developing country resistance to inclusion of services in the new round ultimately crumbled, an overarching bargain had to be struck: old agenda items such as textiles and agriculture were included in the negotiations in exchange for acceptance of the new agenda. (Services were included only as a formally separate set of negotiations, although reporting to a common trade negotiations committee.)[27] In assessing the Uruguay Round outcomes, responses to broader participation in GATT must be placed alongside the deeper integration agenda: the two dynamics intersected throughout the negotiating process.

The Uruguay Round, then, confronted a complex agenda combining traditional elements of protection at the border (although those barriers often reflected entrenched domestic policy regimes) as well as newer items entering the purview of GATT for the first time. Two dimensions of the Uruguay Round outcome are particularly significant in evaluating the institutional corollaries of deeper integration: on the one hand, the GATT response on services, intellectual property rights, and technical standards that touch on policy and regulatory regimes previously viewed as "domestic" and outside GATT scrutiny and, on the other, the institutional changes to GATT itself that were agreed in the negotiations.

GENERAL AGREEMENT ON TRADE IN SERVICES. As Ostry noted, the most contentious items in the Uruguay Round—even those from the old agenda, such as agriculture—"stem from government regulatory policies that were designed to achieve a range of domestic objectives, both economic and noneconomic, with little concern for or recognition of international spillovers."[28] Services, which some members of GATT sought to exclude from the new agenda, are at the core of such policies and conflicts for three reasons: trade in services often includes movement of factors of production (touching on the sensitive issue of foreign investment and right of establishment as well as free movement of labor); service industries are often heavily regu-

27. On the role of smaller trading powers and the developing countries in the Uruguay Round, see Hamilton and Whalley (1988); Winham (1989); Higgott and Cooper (1990).
28. Ostry (1990, p. 17).

lated, a sign of high underlying political stakes; and services are often produced and administered directly by governments, in many economies as regulated or government-owned monopolies.[29] Inclusion of services in the Uruguay Round was in part knowledge driven, requiring a transformation in thinking about services. That transformation, driven by a long-standing and influential expert community, eventually touched even the developing countries. The intellectual shift (linked to and influencing the definition of interests made by powerful actors such as the United States) permitted the application of GATT norms and principles to services in a manner that would have been impossible a decade earlier.[30]

The strategy taken in the General Agreement on Trade in Services (GATS) for dealing with such a politically sensitive array of sectors would be imitated in other parts of the Uruguay Round that dealt with issues bearing on domestic regulatory regimes.[31] The Framework Agreement contained in part II of GATS outlines the "general obligations and disciplines" of all signatories and effectively establishes a broad band of harmonization for national policies in these sectors. The two principal obligations transfer two long-standing GATT norms to the governance of services—nondiscrimination (MFN) and transparency (a broad stipulation on publication of "all relevant measures of general application which pertain to or affect the operation" of the agreement).[32] Transparency requirements similar to those in GATS become an increasingly prominent part of agreements dealing with issues of deeper integration: the impenetrable character of many national regulatory structures and the absence of domestic transparency represent an important first hurdle to entry. Article VI of GATS outlines only very broad obligations regarding domestic regulation of services in addition to MFN and transparency, including procedures and domestic institutions to review administrative decisions affecting the supply of services. Even this apparent reach of GATS rules into domestic regulatory regimes is qualified by an escape clause "where this would be inconsistent with its constitutional structure or the

---

29. Hindley (1990, p. 131).

30. For a detailed account of this transformation, see Drake and Nicolaïdis (1992).

31. This account of GATS and other parts of the Uruguay Round is based on GATT (1994).

32. GATT (1994, article III, p. 329).

nature of its legal system."[33] These broad obligations are subject to specific exemptions (if those exemptions are made known at the time of entry into GATS) and to familiar emergency and balance-of-payments safeguard provisions. The general exceptions that appear in article XX of GATT are transferred to article XIV of GATS, permitting measures directed to a wide range of domestic goals (for example, protecting "human, animal or plant life or health") so long as those exceptions are not discriminatory or a "disguised restriction on trade in services."[34]

These general obligations of GATS are supplemented by specific commitments to national treatment and market access in part III, obligations that are far more significant for most service providers. These obligations are undertaken by countries for particular sectors in national schedules, subject to progressive liberalization through rounds of negotiation (covered in part IV of GATS). GATS establishes an institutional framework that resembles that of other sections of the new WTO: governance through a council and dispute settlement through the dispute settlement understanding (DSU) of the WTO. Finally, a series of sectoral annexes—points of considerable negotiating conflict in the last days of the round—specifies and qualifies the preceding commitments for particular service industries (financial services, maritime transport services, and telecommunications).

At first glance, the general approach of GATS appears even more modest than that of GATT: its general obligations are fewer in number; its escape clauses arguably more numerous. The results for key sectors were disappointing in the eyes of many critics. As Steinberg pointed out, most of the offers made in negotiations conducted on a "request/offer" basis were "insubstantial." It was clear that "many countries simply want to continue protecting their important services sectors."[35] Those countries include the United States in maritime transport and civil aviation and the EU in cultural industries, a major point of conflict at the close of the round. Nevertheless, the GATS form of incorporating a new sector—establishing certain norms that are likely to be accepted by a large number of members

33. GATT (1994, GATS article VI, p. 333).
34. GATT (1994, GATS article XIV, p. 339).
35. Steinberg (1994, pp. 50, 53).

and reserving much of the work of liberalization to the future through plurilateral negotiation—was probably the only workable strategy. As Drake and Nicolaïdis suggested, the text did not dramatically force open national markets for services; "rather, it simply set a framework within which governments could make offers and pressure their counterparts for the same according to common substantive and procedural rules."[36] One key question is whether the widening of liberalization would come, as it had under GATT, through painstaking negotiations on the basis of reciprocity and adherence to the norm of nondiscrimination or whether the threat of suspending MFN treatment (already wielded by the United States) would provide a more effective lever for moving liberalization forward.[37]

AGREEMENT ON TRADE-RELATED ASPECTS OF INTELLECTUAL PROPERTY RIGHTS. This negotiating group was also the site of conflict between the industrialized countries, with a strong interest in harmonization of intellectual property protection to their own tough standards, and the developing countries, technology and information importers who saw few benefits in paying higher rents to the holders of copyrights and patents abroad.[38] As in the case of services, it was not foreordained that GATT would become the site of negotiations on this set of issues: the World Intellectual Property Organization (WIPO), a UN agency, and other multilateral venues existed to coordinate national policies on intellectual property questions; for the industrialized countries, however, a lack of enforcement capabilities rendered these forums increasingly unsatisfactory. The success of GATT negotiations in capturing this issue and successfully forging an agreement resulted from the cross-issue bargains that could be made in GATT (offering concessions to the developing countries on other agenda items to win their agreement on intellectual property), a strategy that was impossible in institutions of narrower scope, such as WIPO. Also, in the course of negotiations, many developing countries were converted to the value of protecting intellectual property rights.[39] As a result, the Trade-Related Aspects of Intellectual Property Rights (TRIPS) Agreement was widely regarded as more suc-

---

36. Drake and Nicolaïdis (1992, p. 91).
37. On this issue, see Steinberg (1994, p. 53).
38. Maskus (1990, pp. 166–69).
39. Frances Williams, "Gatt Joins Battle for Right to Protect," *Financial Times*, July 7, 1994, p. 7.

cessful, with clearer commitments and a stronger enforcement mechanism than the services agreement.

In four respects the TRIPS Agreement illustrates the strengths of GATT and the new WTO in dealing with behind-the-border issues. Following the pattern of GATS, part I of the TRIPS Agreement transfers two familiar principles and commitments from GATT to another realm of international economic exchange: national treatment in the degree of protection afforded intellectual property and an innovative commitment to MFN (any privilege granted to the nationals of any other country is to be accorded "immediately and unconditionally to the nationals of all other members").[40] The agreement also borrows standards of protection from other multilateral agreements governing intellectual property such as the Bern Convention, while making certain key additions such as commercial rentals. Most significant for domestic policy regimes that govern (or fail to govern) intellectual property rights are provisions dealing with procedures and remedies to ensure that intellectual property rights will be enforced. Part III of the agreement contains detailed stipulations regarding the shape of judicial and administrative procedures that will be available to "right holders." These include judicial review of administrative decisions, judicial capabilities to order damages, and "fair and equitable" procedures.[41] In effect, the agreement outlines in considerable detail administrative and judicial guidelines that would transform the protection of intellectual property in many countries. A third advance in the TRIPS Agreement is international enforcement. A fundamental weakness of existing regimes has been the absence of enforcement provisions. Under the TRIPS Agreement, complaints can be lodged under the DSU of the WTO (see below), which, as revised in the Uruguay Round, promises more expeditious enforcement than previous intellectual property regimes. With international enforcement available for the first time, some predict a "rush of disputes" when the new dispute settlement procedures are in place.[42] Finally, to ensure wider participation by the developing countries, the agreement is explicitly multispeed: a lengthy transition period is permitted for developing and transitional economies (five years for

---

40. GATT (1994, TRIPS article 4, pp. 368–69).
41. GATT (1994, pp. 387–92).
42. Williams, "Gatt Joins Battle for Right to Protect."

developing and transitional countries; eleven years for least-developed countries; ten years to provide patent protection if none exists for a particular area of technology).[43]

TRADE-RELATED INVESTMENT MEASURES AGREEMENT.   TRIMs were another prominent target of the United States in the negotiations leading to the launch of the Uruguay Round. In this instance, the extension of GATT principles helped to insert the issue on the agenda but also served to limit the scope of agreement. To the disappointment of those who wished to see the entire panoply of national investment rules open to international negotiation, the TRIMS Agreement remained clearly *trade related*. Evolution in the stance of developing countries toward foreign investment—from hostility and control to active encouragement—during the long Uruguay Round negotiations was key to successful negotiation of even this limited agreement.[44] It has firmly embedded investment within the GATT/WTO institutional edifice and makes it more likely that future investment liberalization will take place under WTO auspices. In sparer form, the TRIMS Agreement mimics the pattern of other behind-the-border issues negotiated in the Uruguay Round by incorporating GATT principles. Members commit to transparency (mandatory notification) and elimination of all TRIMs that are not consistent with GATT articles III (national treatment) and XI (prohibition of quantitative restrictions). Multispeed compliance appears again: developing countries are granted generous transitional periods.

TECHNICAL STANDARDS.   The Agreement on Technical Barriers to Trade and the Agreement on the Application of Sanitary and Phytosanitary Measures provide a final indicator of strategies under GATT for dealing with differences in national regulatory regimes. Technical standards and standards to protect health (in agricultural trade) have been significant barriers to trade and a major point of conflict between those engaged in cross-border exchange and those responsible for any number of legitimate national goals (as well as those seeking protection from imports).

The Standards Code negotiated in the Tokyo Round had already refined the original GATT articles; the two Uruguay Round agreements further elaborated both *strategies* and *principles* for reducing the

43. GATT (1994, articles 65 and 66, pp. 398–99).
44. Graham and Krugman (1990).

negative effects on international trade of divergent national regulatory choices. The two key strategies are harmonization and mutual recognition. Harmonization to international standards becomes the norm in both agreements, unless those standards would be an "ineffective or inappropriate means for the fulfillment of the legitimate objectives pursued."[45] At the same time, mutual recognition is encouraged in the Technical Barriers Agreement if the exporter's regulations "adequately fulfill the objectives" of the importer's regulations and is stipulated in the Sanitary and Phytosanitary Agreement if the exporting member can demonstrate that its measures achieve the desired level of protection.[46]

The two agreements also elaborate principles that can be applied when national standards and regulations appear to restrict the market access of other parties. These principles have become particularly important because standards of this kind are often designed for policy ends that can be defended under the article XX exceptions of GATT. At a time of liberalization and deregulation, regulatory efforts to protect health, consumer safety, and the environment continue to grow: the frontier between these measures and the provisions of GATT has already been politically tense. The principles that emerge from the Uruguay Round negotiations have parallels in the jurisprudence of the European Court of Justice and the American judiciary. Some of the positive principles were present in the original General Agreement— nondiscrimination (MFN) and national treatment; another, the article XX principle that the exceptions listed cannot be deployed as a "disguised restriction on international trade," is a test that is very difficult to use. Determining the intention of a national government (often over its protestations of high-mindedness) may be impossible.

More useful guides appear in these latest agreements. The revised Standards Code proposes a new principle for assessing the "necessity" of a regulation under article XX: "Technical regulations shall not be more trade-restrictive than necessary to fulfill a legitimate objective, taking account of the risks non-fulfillment would create."[47]

45. GATT (1994, Agreement on Technical Barriers to Trade, 2.4, p. 140).

46. GATT (1994, Agreement on Technical Barriers to Trade, 2.7, p. 140; Agreement on the Application of Sanitary and Phytosanitary Measures, article 4, p. 72). Sykes (1995, p. 71) argued that this provision may have the effect of requiring signatories to justify any refusal of mutual recognition.

47. GATT (1994, Agreement on Technical Barriers to Trade, 2.2, p. 139).

The Sanitary and Phytosanitary Agreement adopts further refinements to the principles of the Standards Code: in particular, the need for "scientific justification" if national measures are undertaken to ensure higher levels of protection than those embodied in international standards. Even in such instances, members are enjoined to minimize "negative trade effects."[48] As Sykes suggested, these extensions of GATT principles could lead to intensified international scrutiny of domestic regulatory regimes in the light of their negative effects on trade.[49] The cumulative revision of these GATT principles and their performance post–Uruguay Round should provide useful benchmarks for assessing the international effects of national policies and regulations.

A final institutional innovation in the new Technical Barriers Agreement suggests one avenue for a global regime such as GATT to exert influence over a highly decentralized process such as the setting of technical standards. The agreement extends its reach to the manifold standardizing bodies, governmental and nongovernmental, that have carried out most of the technical standard setting in the past with very little transparency. The new Code of Good Practice for the Preparation, Adoption and Application of Standards is obligatory for central governments, and governments are required to use "reasonable efforts" to obtain compliance from other entities, governmental and nongovernmental, within their jurisdictions.[50] These provisions of the Agreement on Technical Barriers are an innovative attempt to harmonize the harmonizers. If standard-setting organizations accede, this Code of Good Practice, by markedly improving prior notification and transparency, could significantly affect this important range of activities and reduce its trade-inhibiting effects.[51]

STRENGTHENING GATT: DISPUTE SETTLEMENT, SURVEILLANCE, AND THE WTO. Far more than previous GATT negotiations, the Uruguay Round set out to address the perceived institutional weaknesses of GATT. The institutional changes are designed to strengthen *enforcement* through revised dispute settlement procedures, to enhance

---

48. GATT (1994, Agreement on the Application of Sanitary and Phytosanitary Measures, articles 3.3 and 5.4, p. 72).

49. Sykes (1995, pp. 71–72).

50. GATT (1994, Agreement on Technical Barriers, article 4.1, pp. 142–43, and Annex 3, pp. 159–62).

51. Sykes (1995).

the *monitoring* capabilities of the trade regime through a system of multilateral surveillance (the Trade Policy Review Mechanism [TPRM]), and to provide a more *unified and formal institutional frame* for the GATT system by establishing a WTO. The route chosen in this case was constitution making, although some of the innovations were already in place on a provisional basis. (The TPRM, for example, was established at the time of the Uruguay Round midterm review.) In the persistent debate between a political or diplomatic view of GATT as a site for institutionalized discretionary bargaining among states and an alternative view that has argued for moving GATT in a legalized and quasi-judicial direction, it appears that the latter view has gained the upper hand, at least temporarily. The smaller trading states have long been proponents of strengthening GATT; during the Uruguay Round, the United States also became a "hawk" on the strengthening of the DSM, and the threat of American unilateralism moved the other influentials in GATT toward the American view.[52] Typically, the larger trading powers have preferred the political view of GATT; even now, it is far from clear that the United States and the EU are prepared to abandon the instruments of unilateral enforcement in favor of a strengthened GATT. Conditions imposed by the U.S. Senate as the price for its approval of the new WTO—a panel of five federal judges to oversee the outcome of American disputes before the organization—only increased doubts that major trading powers will accept multilateral constraints on their trade policy arsenals.[53]

The revised dispute settlement mechanism deals with one of the major criticisms of enforcement of GATT rulings: the ability of the offending country to delay or block the process at many points through the consensus decision rule. Under the revised DSU, consensus decisionmaking is turned to the advantage of the complainant.[54] The request for a panel can only be refused by consensus; a panel report is adopted by the GATT Council unless it is refused by consensus (or one of the parties indicates its intention to appeal). Because the vindicated party is unlikely to join a consensus to block a

52. Hudec (1990, pp. 186–87).

53. U.S. trade negotiators have claimed that the new dispute settlement understanding allows continued use of section 301, centerpiece of "unfair" trade actions; compare Steinberg (1994, p. 64) to Lowenfeld (1994, p. 481).

54. Details are drawn from GATT (1994, Annex 2, pp. 404–34).

report, the procedures can no longer be stalled by one or another of the interested parties.

The efficiency of the dispute settlement process is also enhanced by the clear time limits that are indicated for each step. If a panel report is not followed by action to correct the offending policies by the government in question and no compensation can be mutually agreed, the dispute settlement body (which governs the procedures) can authorize retaliation (suspension of concessions) by the complaining government. If the level of retaliation is regarded as excessive by the offending party, the new procedures permit binding arbitration to decide the matter; the decision of the arbitrator(s) will be final.

In addition to the dispute settlement procedures designed for violations of GATT rules, a somewhat different set of procedures exists that may be particularly useful for resolving the disputes over the trade consequences of "domestic" policies. Nonviolation complaints, arising from disputes over policies that do not violate GATT rules but do injure the interests of another contracting party, could provide an interesting testing ground for further elaborating GATT norms within this broad and politically sensitive area of ambiguity.[55] The procedures described are simplified, less fraught with penalties, and designed to encourage "a mutually satisfactory adjustment." The offending measure does not have to be withdrawn; even a panel's advice on the needed "adjustment" remains advice and is not binding. Overall, the stakes are much lower for nonviolation complaints, a design that may encourage use of this mechanism for testing the frontiers of international surveillance of apparently domestic policies.

The strengthening of dispute settlement procedures is offset somewhat by additions to the process that permit the parties to intervene along the way (a new "interim review stage" seems to authorize a process of negotiation on the draft panel report between the disputants and the panel members) and to appeal the legal grounding of a panel report to a new standing appellate body. These additional hedges necessarily lengthen the time elapsed between the initial complaint and final adoption of the panel report. Nevertheless, the overall

55. Article 26 of Annex 2 of the DSU describes these procedures; see GATT (1994, pp. 427–28).

effect of the revisions in the DSM is to create a "substantial strengthening" of rule-based procedures under GATT.[56]

The TPRM, created in 1989 and incorporated in the Uruguay Round results, enhances the transparency of national commercial policies by establishing for the first time a means to monitor those policies in their entirety.[57] Reports on national trade policies are prepared by the GATT secretariat and by the country and reviewed by the trade policy review body. The TPRM appears to be modeled closely on the article IV consultations carried out by the IMF with its members. Such exercises provide an opportunity for inducing compliance with GATT (WTO) rules through peer pressure on the basis of increased information. The enhanced transparency produced by these regularized policy reviews is complemented by a reaffirmation of the requirement to notify adoption of trade measures "affecting the operation of GATT 1994." After the Uruguay Round, the secretariat will establish a "central registry" of these notifications, which will be available to the other contracting parties.[58] Although legalists have argued that the TPRM might "divert attention from the legal norms in such a way as actually to decrease the pressure on Contracting Parties to observe those norms" and encourage the (misguided) view that GATT is a "'negotiating' or 'consulting' organization," the TPRM appears to provide an additional channel for members to enforce those norms through more informal means.[59] Above all, it reduces the costs to members of monitoring opaque national trade policy regimes.

The final institutional innovation of the Uruguay Round is the creation of a WTO to supersede and incorporate not only GATT but also the other agreements and protocols that have been negotiated in the round and in earlier negotiations. The WTO adds weight and permanence to the institutions governing international trade and offsets the fragmentation through plurilateralism that has characterized the international trade regime since at least the Tokyo Round. The new organization raises the political profile of commercial policy, particularly when trade negotiations are not under way, by organizing

---

56. Price (1992, pp. 92–95); for other evaluations of the revised DSM: Pescatore (1993, pp. 17–19); Castel (1989, pp. 843–48); Lowenfeld (1994).
57. The TPRM is described in Annex 3. See GATT (1994, pp. 434–37).
58. GATT (1994, pp. 444–45).
59. The legalist critique is found in Jackson (1990, p. 80).

a meeting of top trade officials on a biennial schedule (or more frequently). To the new WTO is also delegated the task of strengthening relations with the other principal international economic institutions, particularly the Bretton Woods organizations. Overall, the WTO will not create new obligations or rules: it merely serves as a coherent frame for housing a multiplicity of trade agreements (including GATT) and a centralized dispute settlement mechanism. It does, however, have two very important concrete effects. Those who wish to join the WTO must accede not only to the components of GATT 94 but also to such new agreements as GATS and TRIPS. Only four relatively minor agreements are optional.[60] This bargain for membership in the WTO resembles "fast-track" authority in the American trade arena: prospective members must accept or reject the whole trade regime. Put another way, the trade regime may be multispeed, but it is not à la carte.

The WTO also unifies dispute settlement procedures for the various trade agreements. This raises the possibility that enforcement may involve suspension of concessions (retaliation) across agreements and issue-areas. For example, a country found in violation of its obligations under the TRIPS Agreement could face suspension of concessions under GATT 94. This ability to link issue-areas could strengthen the enforcement powers of the new DSU (although the effective importance of enforcement in dispute settlement in the past has been small).

The GATT that has emerged from the Uruguay Round is an institution whose trajectory has confounded the predictions of many of its critics. GATT is not "dead," as some have argued: its scope has been enlarged, its organizational profile sharpened, and its monitoring and enforcement capabilities strengthened. Certainly its enlargement in scope is owed in part to the issues of deeper integration—the turbulent frontier of domestic policy regimes and international rules—but equally to the widening of GATT to become a genuinely global organization. The logic of the Uruguay Round and its outcomes were driven in large measure by conflict between the industrialized great powers of the trade regime whose minilateral deals had previously dominated governance of the regime and the emerging trading states of the developing world, increasingly dependent on

60. Lowenfeld (1994, pp. 478–79).

uncertain access to the markets of North America, Europe, and Japan. The industrialized powers were unwilling to accept free riders on several key issues; the developing economies were insistent on dealing with the old agenda of trade protectionism and (together with the smaller industrialized economies) intent on curbing the unilateralism of their bigger trading partners.

Trade Regime and Economic Integration: New Issues, New Institutions

GATT has been widely criticized as a weak institution unable to police national policies, lacking a clear organizational core, and based on rules that were riddled with exceptions. Its evolution reflected the hesitations of its principal members when ceding influence over politically sensitive commercial policy. GATT developed as a patchwork of agreements, codes, and dispute settlement outcomes; it presided over a fragmented trade regime, one in which bilateralism and negotiations outside GATT (and counter to GATT principles) persisted. Nevertheless, its members chose to deal with many contentious behind-the-border issues within GATT. Its proponents hoped that the strengthened GATT that seemed to emerge from the Uruguay Round would continue to deal with new agenda items as they arose in the world economy. The widened scope of GATT after the Uruguay Round indicated that it would become the global institution that grappled with conflicts between the desire for expanded international exchange and the desire for national autonomy.

That optimism was tempered by an awareness of GATT's past institutional design and the ways in which its changed character as the WTO might affect its role. The Uruguay Round was a cumbersome affair, in part because GATT's large and increasingly heterogeneous membership combined with a consensus decisionmaking to make GATT a less-than-efficient setting for collective action. Its broad scope did make it easier to strike bargains across issues that actively engaged the developing countries in trade negotiations. The new WTO hardly dealt with these obstacles to GATT effectiveness through institutional devices such as delegation or representation. Concern with negotiation gridlock in an ever-expanding WTO lends caution to proposals for a new trade round in the near future.

In dealing with a series of contentious issues on the frontier of domestic policy choice and expanded international trade and investment, the reasons for GATT's success need to be clarified. Those who applauded the centralized and formal structure of the new WTO often overlook the value of the decentralized and flexible GATT which had adapted (with substantial lags) to new circumstances in the world economy. The openness and fragmentation of GATT as an institution permitted a high degree of flexibility in meeting its members' demands. New issues that had never been seen as "trade-related" were incorporated in negotiations; environmental issues were also placed on the GATT agenda with relative ease. GATT principles and obligations proved to be readily transferable to sectors beyond trade as conventionally defined, and GATT criteria for examining domestic policies that conflicted with market access were rapidly disseminated to other trade fora. It is not clear that a more centralized, formal, and rule-based institution would have proved so robust and adaptable to changing world economic circumstances.

In any case, strengthened institutions in the new WTO still faced several tests. The WTO might fail to capture a larger proportion of trade disputes in the new DSM. The new procedures did not deal directly with the reluctance of many smaller countries to lodge complaints against their more powerful trading partners. Despite greater efficiency and more reliable enforcement, the DSM could lapse into disuse, as it had at other points in the history of GATT. Stronger might not mean more effective in the eyes of its members, whatever their enthusiasm at the close of the Uruguay Round. Whatever the future of the WTO, however, GATT, stepchild of postwar economic institutions, had demonstrated that a history of incremental and piecemeal growth, an appearance of weak influence over its members, of agreements and codes that often appeared cobbled together in a less-than-coherent whole, did not prevent it from dealing with a diverse new economic agenda and many new members through innovation and incorporation.

The IMF: Financial Integration, Rules, and Coordination

The Bretton Woods monetary regime shared one institutional feature with GATT—the absence of a secure domestic anchorage within the politics of its member states—but on most other dimensions of institutional variation, it was firmly planted at one end: a formal, rule-based monetary regime with an organizational core, the IMF, that possessed, at least on paper, substantial powers of monitoring and enforcement. Formed by an intergovernmental agreement whose core rules were not substantially revised for three decades, the Bretton Woods regime was intended to be global in membership—only the communist bloc countries absented themselves. Those who believe that the most efficient means of international policy coordination are highly institutionalized, rule-based systems still portray the Bretton Woods system as a golden age. Yet its principal features crumbled in part because of increased international financial integration, and the role of the IMF in subsequent episodes of international economic policy coordination has been marginal. Instead, wielding the instrument of conditionality, the Bretton Woods institutions have served as a means of integrating poorer and newer members of the capitalist economy (wider integration) rather than dealing with the coordination of economic policies among the industrialized countries. By the 1990s the central role of the IMF was the linkage of financial support to international oversight of the domestic policy regimes of developing countries and, most recently, the ex-socialist economies.

Bretton Woods System: Policy Coordination in an Era of Shallow Integration

Although the post-1945 monetary regime possessed a centralized monitoring mechanism lacking in GATT, in other respects national policies were coordinated in a decentralized manner. National governments made policy choices in the context of internationally agreed-upon rules governing exchange rates and foreign exchange restrictions. Like GATT in the era of shallow integration, a distinction between "external" and "domestic" policies was drawn. Rules were directed to constraining certain mutually harmful external policies, in particular preventing competitive depreciation and restrictions on current account convertibility. The idea of central policy coordination bargains was not part of the Bretton Wood scheme.[61]

Although the Bretton Woods system is often represented as a strong, rule-based institution, the role of the IMF in sustaining stable exchange rates and beneficial economic outcomes remains unclear.

61. Crockett (1989, p. 347).

For some observers, the Bretton Woods system was an important constraint on domestic policies; for others, the clarity of the IMF's injunctions and its enforcement capabilities are belied by the record. Familiar issues of measuring compliance and assessing the IMF's role in changing the behavior of national governments arise here, as they did in evaluating GATT's DSMs. Concessions to domestic policy autonomy were embedded in the rules themselves and in their application. Although the Articles of Agreement obliged members to maintain fixed par values, those values could be adjusted, an element of advance over the gold standard's "rigidity" that constituted the principal novelty of the regime in the opinion of its architects.[62] Although the exchange rate system became less adjustable and more fixed over time, IMF monitoring and enforcement seemed to play a minor role in this outcome. A member was required to consult with the IMF when a parity change was declared for reasons of "fundamental disequilibrium" (itself an ambiguous criterion). Although the Fund could sanction a member that undertook such a change over its objections, such sanctions were imposed only once early in the history of the regime (France in 1948, to little effect). Later, major countries often changed their exchange rates without notifying the IMF. One industrialized country, Canada, floated its exchange rate from 1950 to 1962, and the IMF imposed no sanctions. The record on multiple exchange rates was equally spotty: as late as 1962, fifteen of eighty-two members of the IMF had multiple rates. The second major prohibition of the regime—exchange controls on current account transactions—was eased by a lengthy transition period before full convertibility was required.[63]

Despite evidence that the IMF was not an agent of rule enforcement, the record of the Bretton Woods system on exchange rates is relatively clear: although major adjustments did take place, "during the so-called heyday of the Bretton Woods era, 1959–67, most developed countries did maintain stable and convertible exchange rates."[64] Given the apparent record of compliance and enforcement, one would need to demonstrate a difficult counterfactual—that more

---

62. Black (1991, p. 107).
63. The record of compliance and enforcement is drawn from Dam (1982, pp. 129–33, 159–65); see Bordo (1993, pp. 46–47); Dominguez (1993, pp. 378–82).
64. Dominguez (1993, p. 382).

"undesirable" exchange rate changes would have taken place without the Bretton Woods regime—to confirm an important role for the IMF.[65] Alternative explanations include the buoyant international economic conditions of these years (to which the Bretton Woods system may have contributed): adjustment to exchange rate rules was less politically painful, and the economic costs (in terms of lost output) were low.

Bretton Woods was a regime of both "rules and reputation": reputational considerations, international and domestic, deterred temptations to defect from the exchange rate regime.[66] Cooperation under Bretton Woods was linked to cooperation in other issue-areas: threats to the monetary regime were often portrayed as threats to the larger pattern of international collaboration. Peer pressure in other arenas of consultation, such as the OECD's Working Party 3, reinforced these reputational concerns. For some countries, such as Japan, exchange rate parity seemed to symbolize national identity as a law-abiding state. Exchange rate rules also sealed domestic distributional bargains: depreciation or appreciation could impose costs on coalition members, particularly in open economies, and thereby threaten electoral defeat.[67]

Acceptance of exchange rate constraints was promoted by two other features of the Bretton Woods institutions. Although financial assistance had been mobilized by central banks under the gold standard, such efforts had been ad hoc and often unreliable. The ability of the IMF to mobilize financial support for beleaguered currencies and adjustment programs was a crucial break with the past. Through conditionality—an exchange of finance for specified policy changes— the IMF (and the principal financial powers) also obtained a means of influencing policies that might have been considered beyond its purview. The negotiation and monitoring of IMF standby arrangements resulted in institutional strengthening through delegation from the member governments to the staff and managing director of the Fund. The provision of finance was supplemented by acquiescence in national capital controls. Although the IMF and its policy advice typically tilted in a liberalizing direction (removal of exchange controls,

---

65. For a related argument see Alesina (1993, p. 400).
66. Oudiz and Sachs (1984).
67. Kahler (1988).

for example), cross-border capital flows were viewed as destabilizing. In this case, national autonomy was not prohibited but permitted. The distancing of the new regime—anchored in national treasuries—from the central banks and private financiers that had operated the gold standard was apparent in this deviation from liberal norms.

Two institutional alternatives for organizing the international monetary order had preceded the government-negotiated rules that made up the Bretton Woods system: "great power" collaboration in a system of discretionary bargaining and central bank cooperation linked to liberalized private finance, the institutional underpinnings of the gold standard. By the 1960s, both of these alternatives to the IMF-centered system were demonstrating renewed appeal. The need to mobilize additional financing for industrialized country borrowers led to swap arrangements under the Bank for International Settlements (BIS), the central bankers' club. Targeted for abolition at Bretton Woods, the BIS had survived and prospered as a key player in European monetary affairs. Its resilient institutional alternative was strengthened by close regulatory links to burgeoning financial markets.

More immediately apparent was the growing role of the Group of Ten (G-10), industrialized countries who negotiated the General Arrangements to Borrow outside the IMF and available only to its members. This grouping found somewhat different form in Working Party 3 of the OECD. Although the IMF awarded a dominant position to the industrialized countries through weighted voting (unlike the consensus rule of GATT), collaboration among the industrialized countries outside the IMF would become an increasingly familiar pattern in international monetary affairs during the 1960s. Even before the breakdown of the par value system, "the system was managed by the United States in cooperation with other members of the G-10."[68] In part the growing membership of developing countries in the IMF made such alternatives more attractive to the rich countries; in part such plurilateralism reflected a desire for more explicit policy coordination among economies that were characterized by goods and capital markets that were increasingly integrated. If a principal role of the IMF was information exchange, then each of these institutional options

68. Bordo (1993, pp. 73–74).

could play that role more efficiently for the most powerful members of the system.[69]

Explanations for the collapse of the rule-based Bretton Woods exchange rate system have centered on four elements of the regime: changes in knowledge, national preferences driven by domestic political constraints (particularly in the United States), the erosion of capital controls, leading to rapid growth in cross-border capital flows, and the inherent weaknesses of a rule-based monetary order. The influence of Keynesian ideas grew in western Europe simultaneously with the embrace of flexible or floating exchange rates in the United States: both demoted exchange rate stability when it conflicted with other economic objectives. The government of the United States, the anchor in the system, was particularly unwilling to forgo the domestic political penalties required if the exchange rate could not be used as a policy instrument. In a setting of fixed exchange rates, growing capital mobility meant that autonomous national monetary policies were increasingly untenable. Under changed conditions, the Bretton Woods system did not have "constitutional conventions" (unlike the later European Monetary System) for triggering negotiations to establish new parities; instead, as established parities came under increasing pressure, a contest between the United States and the Europeans ensued to determine who would bear the burden of adjustment. Inability to strike a coordinated bargain on exchange rates was duplicated in the coordination of monetary policy: growing capital mobility under fixed exchange rates implied loss of control over national monetary policies, but coordination on that front was equally difficult, given political constraints. The immediate result of greater capital market integration was pressure on a rule-based system of monetary governance and its ultimate transformation into an even more decentralized regime of flexible exchange rates with weakened core rules.

Institutional Variation and Policy Coordination

Failure to reconstruct a modified fixed exchange rate regime in the early 1970s produced a "nonsystem" in the eyes of some observers. The second amendment to the Articles of Agreement of the IMF

69. On the informational role of the IMF, see Dominguez (1993, p. 391); Eichengreen (1993, pp. 642–43).

restated national obligations in the new circumstances. Choice of an exchange rate regime was now a purely national choice—"mutual recognition" of exchange rate policies. Under the new article IV, members were obligated only to "collaborate with the Fund and other members to assure orderly exchange arrangements and to promote a stable system of exchange rates." These requirements were interpreted to mean no manipulation of exchange rates (continuing the old norm against competitive devaluations) and, more broadly, the pursuit of stable domestic economic policies.[70]

The IMF's role in overseeing these obligations was captured in the concept of surveillance: narrowly defined to encompass scrutiny of exchange rate policies, and more broadly defined to extend the Fund's monitoring to include previously "domestic" policies.[71] As Crockett pointed out, the lack of strong policy guidelines for governments, and particularly the absence of clear exchange rate rules, led to the elaboration of new consultation mechanisms overseen by the IMF: "In the absence of clear guidance on what were considered inappropriate policies, the Fund itself would have to provide the analysis and rationale for potentially sensitive judgments about members' policies."[72] Mechanisms of surveillance included regular article IV consultations with members of the Fund on their national economic policies and the World Economic Outlook exercise, which provided a benchmark for projections about the international economic environment.[73] Unless a member requested financial support from the IMF (and no industrial country turned to the Fund for a stand-by arrangement after 1977), the new surveillance procedures appeared relatively ineffectual in changing national policies. Annual discussion of reports on article IV consultations provided only an opportunity for modest peer group pressure on national policymakers. The fact that the reports remained confidential meant that international oversight did not feed readily into the domestic political

70. Crockett (1989, p. 352).
71. The new understanding of surveillance was adopted by the executive board in 1977. On the concept of surveillance, see Dam (1982, pp. 266–67); Pauly (1992); Kahler (1988).
72. Crockett (1989, p. 354).
73. Crockett (1989, p. 354). As Crockett noted, a process of special consultation to deal with questions regarding particular countries was seldom used (two countries in the first ten years). Also, the executive board was given notice and analysis of major changes in exchange rates between consultations.

process. A bad "report card" from the Fund would never become part of domestic political debate unless published by the government itself; domestic political bargains and commitments did not reinforce the international rules of the game.

The transformed monetary regime did not provide the degree of domestic policy autonomy that theory had promised; an awareness of spillover effects and a desire for greater exchange rate stability brought calls for more explicit policy coordination in place of the modest consultation and harmonization that occurred under the IMF. For those arguing for a more centralized system of policy coordination, exchange rate stability was portrayed as a public good that was likely to be underprovided in a decentralized system. Also, volatility and misalignment of exchange rates could produce policy spillovers of a different sort: threats of protectionism and capital controls to counter disorder in the exchange rate system. According to these rationales, coordination of national policies could produce a global economic outcome superior to that under more decentralized management.[74]

Despite its new role in the surveillance of its members' policies, the IMF was peripheral to attempts at economic policy coordination that emerged among the industrialized countries. During the 1960s the activities of Working Party 3 in the OECD had first recognized the importance of externalities in economic adjustment. Its *Report on the Balance of Payments Adjustment Process* in 1966 "implicitly recognized that this role [in policy coordination] had to go beyond monitoring compliance with a set of agreed international obligations."[75] This pattern of negotiating on policy coordination outside the IMF persisted, and two settings for discretionary bargaining emerged in the 1970s and 1980s. One, politician-centered, was situated in the annual economic summits; the second, the G-5/G-7 process, began with meetings among finance ministers and their deputies and was gradually and weakly institutionalized in the late 1980s. In both cases, the cycle of policy coordination was driven by the U.S. government: as the most closed among the major industrialized economies, the United States typically pursued a course of policy autonomy until domestic political costs rose (inflation in the late 1970s and protec-

---

74. Frenkel, Goldstein, and Masson (1991, pp. 18–20).
75. Crockett (1989, p. 349).

tionism in the mid-1980s); it then turned to a collective mechanism to reduce those costs (often interpreted by its partners as simple pressure to relieve the burdens of adjustment on the United States and serve as reluctant "locomotives" for the world economy).

The economic summits evolved from informal meetings of the G-5 finance ministers (the Library Group) and were initially modeled on those gatherings: self-consciously informal and lacking in institutional underpinning. During the late 1970s greater staff involvement in preparation for the summits and more extensive links to the national bureaucracies and international institutions were constructed, but the thickening of domestic linkages and construction of institutional regularities faded in the early 1980s. Although Putnam and Bayne argued that capabilities for coordinating policies declined from the 1970s to the 1980s, any assessment is difficult, because the universe of successful cases is so small. Only one summit, the Bonn Summit of 1978, is a clear exemplar of explicit policy coordination—mutual adjustment of economic policies to achieve a superior joint outcome.[76] Two significant benefits are apparent in the politician-centered model: the ability to make cross-issue bargains and the added credibility of any agreement reached by the top political leaders. The commitment of the senior political leadership could also ease implementation after a bargain is struck.

The summits were used less often as the principal site of coordination for several reasons. Disagreements over underlying models of international economic interaction and national economic performance could not easily be resolved in a setting that was only weakly institutionalized: a common technical analysis is often required to bridge such differences. Although top politicians could construct bargains across issues and bureaucracies, they were less likely to do so without support from a "conspiracy of internationalists" (Putnam and Bayne) such as the one that produced the Bonn Summit bargain. Such a transgovernmental coalition required the intimate involvement of key bureaucracies in the preparation and management of the summits. The agenda of the summits became more diffuse and laden with high-politics issues as the new cold war opened in the 1980s.[77]

76. On the economic summits, see Putnam and Bayne (1987); on the Bonn summit, see Putnam and Henning (1989); Holtham (1989).
77. On the advantages and disadvantages of the summit model, see Kahler (1988, pp. 388–90).

After a period of diminished interest in economic policy coordination, however, a new locus in the G-5/G-7, linked to the summits and to the IMF surveillance process, took shape in the late 1980s.

The Versailles Summit (1982) authorized new institutional links that were portrayed at first as an aid to policy convergence on anti-inflationary goals, not as a first step toward policy coordination. In the new procedures of multilateral surveillance, the managing director of the IMF would meet regularly with the G-5 finance ministers. The new pattern of coordination was only confirmed, however, when driven by changing American personnel and politics in 1985. The Plaza accord (1985) was followed by an agreement at the Tokyo Summit (May 1986) that endorsed multilateral surveillance, expanded it to the G-7 and included the IMF in the surveillance exercise, and delegated the process to the finance ministers and their deputies. The Louvre Accord of February 1987 marked the peak of policy and exchange rate commitments in the new phase of policy coordination. After a further year of preparation, performance indicators for the multilateral surveillance process were approved at the Venice Summit.[78]

The process of economic policy coordination that evolved after 1985 had no formal institutions at its core: the G-7 ministerial meetings have no formal chair and no secretariat. The IMF informally assumed some of the roles of a secretariat, providing technical assistance and an objective source of advice to the G-7 meetings; it also offered the voice of its members outside the G-7. IMF management and staff were involved in developing surveillance indicators and providing analytic support, but they were excluded from discussions of foreign exchange market issues.[79] The effort to move modestly in the direction of a rule-based system based on broad reference ranges for exchange rates was not successful: the ranges were gradually broadened and provided little credibility to government policy commitments. The degree of constraint on government policies exercised by the ranges was minimal. Peer group pressure was equally ineffective; when it was explicitly used, it met with only "mixed success."[80]

78. Dobson (1991, pp. 39–47); see also Funabashi (1988).

79. Dobson (1991, pp. 32, 36); Crockett (1989, p. 356).

80. On these difficulties with the G-7 process, see Dobson (1991, pp. 70–71, 73–75, 102, 117).

Evaluating the record of economic policy coordination after 1985 requires answers to the same difficult counterfactual questions raised for the IMF under Bretton Woods. Although economic performance improved after 1985 on certain measures (narrowing of exchange rate misalignment, lowering of external imbalances), the contribution of the G-7 policy coordination process to these outcomes is unclear. Dobson awarded highest marks for crisis management, the "telephone accord" of late 1987 that limited the risks that the sharp stock market declines would become an economic crisis. In other areas, Dobson suggested that market-induced adjustment would have been both more rapid and more disruptive than the G-7-managed outcomes. Overall, however, pressure from other industrialized countries at best "nudges along" policies already in train for domestic reasons. International influence on economic policy choice, at least for the major industrialized countries, remains slight. Since 1985 the industrialized countries have constructed "an elaborate institutional framework, but one that has not developed into a real mechanism for economic policy coordination."[81]

As Ralph Bryant suggested, one can read the record of economic policy coordination as one indicative of deficiencies given the collective goods that were forgone, or one could evaluate it as demonstrating a surprising level of activism given the obstacles.[82] For those who argue that more effective coordination would produce measurable gains, three linked diagnoses are offered for improvement: improvements in knowledge about international interactions (spillovers) and national economies, international institution building, and domestic political change.

One critical piece of knowledge that can shape commitments to coordination is the scale of the gains from coordination. Most attention has been devoted to explicit coordination, which has been rare; estimates of potential gains are not high. Although Bryant argued that the "jury is still out," Fischer's judgment, that "the gains from coordination per se would be small, even if the correct model of the economy is known," is shared by many.[83] More disturbing is the finding of McKibbin and Sachs that coordination of both fiscal and

---

81. Dobson (1991, p. 76).
82. Bryant (forthcoming).
83. Bryant (forthcoming); Fischer (1988, p. 23).

monetary policy produces much larger gains than monetary policy alone: the most intractable policy instrument is necessary for the greatest gains.[84] Even with less ambitious models of coordination, however, information exchange can reduce both model uncertainty and uncertainty regarding the likely behavior of other governments. Such uncertainty has clearly raised significant obstacles to otherwise valuable (in the eyes of policymakers) policy coordination.[85] The structure of G-7 coordination, which awards a prominent role to such information sharing, suggests its value for national policymakers.

Information about national policies or improved knowledge of international economic spillovers is also linked directly to institution building. One widespread criticism of the G-7 process is the absence of adequate analytical support in the form of a clearly designated secretariat, a unit that could most easily be located in the IMF or another existing international organization.[86] Such an institution (or institutional addition) could also serve to connect the macroeconomic policy coordination process to other issue-areas, such as GATT and trade policy (a desideratum already signaled in the conclusion of the Uruguay Round).

Apart from the link between international institutions and information exchange and knowledge enhancement, the role that additional institutionalization could usefully play in economic policy coordination is unclear. Despite the portrayal of policy coordination as a collaboration game in some of the theoretical literature, defection from agreed bargains or commitments has probably been exaggerated. The need for international institutions to monitor such commitments does not loom large in actual practice. As Putnam and Henning noted, in the case of summit bargains, reputational and cross-issue barriers to cheating are relatively strong and obviate the need for powerful international institutions. The "visibility and solemnity of the commitment, its verifiability, the frequency of dealing among the contracting parties, the value that they attribute to those other deals, and the number of other parties 'observing' the game" all argue against widespread reneging from policy coordination bargains.[87]

84. McKibbin and Sachs (1991, p. 187).
85. Weatherford (1988, p. 635).
86. Dobson (1991, p. 145); see also Bryant (forthcoming).
87. Putnam and Henning (1989, p. 102).

More serious, however, are the weaknesses in the linkages between existing institutional arrangements and the domestic politics of cooperating states. These weaknesses can produce considerable slippage in implementing agreements. Tension between the finance ministries, which were dominant in the G-7 process, and the more independent central banks had to be overcome to fulfill G-7 bargains.[88] The fading involvement of political principals after 1985 meant that gains in technical and analytic power have been made at the cost of greater political credibility for commitments made. As noted above, constructing closer ties to the political level would also permit cross-issue bargaining and favor the forging of transnational coalitions. The success of the Bonn coordination bargain rested on divided governments: such divisions will not be evident in a process dominated by one national bureaucracy and one that is normally sensitive to its political masters. Each of these arguments for expanding the domestic anchorage of economic policy coordination, however, could require significant internal changes within participating states. In economic policy coordination and other issue-areas, as economic integration advances, more bureaucratic players must be engaged to implement international bargains. In the absence of high-level political commitments, international monitoring of those bargains within national political systems becomes more important, more costly, and usually less effective. Devising institutional means to accomplish these new and difficult tasks is one key to the success of international collaboration.

The IMF in an Era of Deeper and Wider Integration

The IMF and the rule-based exchange rate system that it represented did not fare well in an era of increasing capital mobility and financial integration. If Barry Eichengreen's analysis is correct, the reconstruction of a rule-based system in a setting absent capital controls will be difficult or impossible: capital mobility poses starker choices for governments, a choice between floating exchange rates or monetary union.[89] In its place, for the past two decades, the IMF has overseen a modest system of surveillance over exchange rate manipulation and national economic policies. Based on consultation, the

---

88. Dobson (1991, pp. 137–39).
89. Eichengreen (1994, p. 78).

boundaries placed on national policy autonomy by IMF surveillance have been very wide, and peer pressure has served as the only means of enforcement. As the IMF's membership grew and became more diverse in the 1960s, a second alternative for monetary collaboration among the industrialized countries emerged—settings in which the scrutiny of the developing countries would be absent. First the G-10 and the OECD's Working Party 3, later the G-5, the economic summits, and the G-7 served as negotiating arenas for policy coordination. The IMF was gradually drawn into the latest version of this episodic and discretionary mode of bargaining, but its role was limited to that of a quasi secretariat, not the central one that the founders at Bretton Woods had awarded it. In certain respects, the modest ambitions of G-7 collaboration did not require the strong organizational core represented by the IMF. At best, the IMF could become a more clear-cut center for information sharing and analytical support, providing "an agreed data base, an impartial source of analysis, and the necessary staff resources to prepare supporting material on a continuous basis."[90]

Global financial integration undermined the rule-based monetary system of Bretton Woods. It also undercut the principal instrument of influence exercised by the IMF to influence national economic policies: financial resources offered conditionally. For believers in the power of private markets, the emerging global financial markets served as the only "discipline" necessary for errant national governments: rather than a cartel of other national governments coaxing one of its fellows to change direction, thousands of private economic agents would deliver the message more insistently and effectively. Private financial markets also provided a ready source of financial resources as an alternative to the IMF, undermining its bargaining position. Even middle-income developing countries in the 1970s were able to turn away from the Fund in a period of financial plenty. Only the onset of the debt crisis in 1982 and the rapid decline in private financial flows reestablished the IMF's crucial position as a last-resort source of financing for the heavily indebted developing countries.[91] The debt crisis had a second effect. The architects of the postwar monetary regime, reacting against both the gold standard and the

90. Crockett (1989, p. 362).
91. For an account of the IMF role in the debt crisis, see Sachs (1988).

power of private financiers, had purposely constructed an organization that would serve as the agent of governments. The central bank network of cooperation centered on the BIS had remained distant from the Fund, and the IMF had few direct links to the burgeoning international financial markets. The debt crisis of necessity produced a working relationship between the IMF and private bankers; because central banks were directly concerned with the safety and soundness of their national financial systems, their links to the IMF grew as well. IMF analytical capabilities in monitoring private financial markets improved.

Even before the onset of the debt crisis, IMF conditionality had been slowly evolving from exclusively short-term stand-by arrangements focused on monetary and fiscal instruments toward longer-term programs that emphasized "structural" changes in the policy regime of the program country. Under pressure from the developing countries, the IMF had initiated the extended fund facility in 1974 to provide programs with more substantial resources over a longer period of time. In the 1980s, two additional facilities were directed toward low-income developing countries, the structural adjustment facility and the enhanced structural adjustment facility; a third, the systemic transformation facility, was created for the formerly planned economies of the Soviet bloc. The conditionality associated with these programs included provisions regarding the trade regime, public sector reform, and pricing policy, as well as the more familiar fiscal and monetary policy instruments.[92] At approximately the same time (the early 1980s), the World Bank began to move away from its concentration on project lending toward structural adjustment and sectoral adjustment loans that took an economywide perspective and also included broad programs of policy reform that extended well beyond purely macroeconomic instruments.[93] More recently, goals of poverty alleviation have assumed a more prominent role in conditionality, and there have been demands, particularly in the United States, for including environmental requirements in programs as well. The composition of government expenditures, and particularly the share awarded to military expenditures, has come under increasing scrutiny by both

---

92. Polak (1991, pp. 6–8).
93. On World Bank lending, see Mosley, Harrigan, and Toye (1991); Corbo (1991).

the World Bank and the IMF.[94] Although both international institutions have managed to exclude political conditions from their programs, national aid programs are now taking human rights and democratization goals into account in devising program conditionality.

This role in influencing policy change is concerned neither with the policy spillovers produced by economic integration among the industrialized countries nor with the clash of national policy regimes, the issues of deeper integration. For nearly two decades, the IMF's lending has been directed exclusively to the developing and ex-socialist economies. In the case of the IMF and World Bank, and to a degree GATT, the role delegated to the global institutions by the major economic powers is one of wider integration: liberalizing trade regimes, ending price controls, and reforming public sector enterprises may include a certain degree of policy harmonization, but they only set the stage for further economic integration. Most contemporary clients of the Bretton Woods organizations, however, confront marginalization in world markets, not intensified integration.

As IMF and World Bank conditionality has intruded on policy areas that were once reserved as sovereign or domestic, however, their record does offer one caution to other institutions seeking to effect change from the outside.[95] Tests of government commitment to the policy changes become important devices for determining the likelihood of successful implementation. Monitoring compliance is far more difficult when the policies in question extend beyond macroeconomic policies. As the range of policies and agencies affected by conditionality grows, the allowable lag between an expected policy action and the outcome that is used to measure compliance lengthens.[96] More important, a bargaining model based simply on monitoring and enforcement does not adequately explain the success and failure of conditionality. Instead, a strategy of establishing significant domestic linkages—political allies that will persist over time—often offers a higher probability of success in influencing national policies. Technical assistance creates institutions and reli-

94. Polak (1991, pp. 24–33).
95. On the knotty issue of measuring external influence, see Kahler (1992, pp. 95–101).
96. Mosley (1987, p. 2).

able interlocutors to staff them. Policy dialogues between the IMF and national governments have also served to establish greater agreement on the underlying model of both the international and domestic economies.[97]

The outpouring of advice and admonition that has marked the fiftieth anniversary of the IMF and the World Bank sets out several alternative futures for these global institutions. Critics on the left, convinced that the Bretton Woods organizations perpetuate poverty and environmental degradation, and skeptics on the right, who counsel reliance on private financial markets, urge simple abolition of these institutions. Those who do not recommend this drastic alternative suggest one of two futures. A return to first principles marks the recommendations of the Bretton Woods Commission: restoring the IMF to its place at the center of international monetary affairs and linking it securely to "a more formal system of coordination" among the industrialized countries, one that aims at stabilizing exchange rates.[98] To this end, institutional reforms are recommended: strengthening the direction given by the interim committee, elevating the executive directors, and creating an advisory committee to provide expertise on the international financial system.[99] Unfortunately, these prescriptions for policy coordination do not address all the explanations for its lackluster record: inadequate institutions were only one. Other observers, more pessimistic that the major economies will permit a stiffened process of policy coordination, accept the present role of the IMF in widening international economic integration. Its future then becomes that of the "disappearing residual": attending to financing and policy advice for the poorest developing countries and transitional economies that lack access to the private financial markets and disbanding when that access is achieved.[100] A third prospect has received less attention: the inadequacies of plurilateral monetary cooperation as economies outside the G-7 grow in importance. Just as the GATT serves to prevent free riding by smaller traders, the IMF

97. On these influence techniques and their strengths and weaknesses, see Kahler (1992, pp. 123–33).

98. Bretton Woods Commission (1994, pp. 4–5).

99. Bretton Woods Commission (1994, p. 6).

100. See, for example, Martin Wolf, "Bretton Twins at an Awkward Age," *Financial Times*, October 7, 1994, p. 17.

may be able to incorporate new financial and monetary powers into a system of consultation and coordination that reaches beyond the present industrialized country club.

Global Regulatory Regimes in an Era of Market Integration and Liberalization

GATT and the IMF were only the most prominent global institutions that confronted political conflicts and institutional demands imposed by economic integration. Technological change and demands for domestic deregulation challenged global regulatory regimes more directly, disrupting secure international bargains and stimulating the search for new regulatory structures. Two of the three cases discussed here demonstrate the importance of shifts in knowledge and expert communities that were crucial in fracturing a previous regulatory consensus. In each of the cases—telecommunications, banking, and environmental protection—outcomes were deeply influenced by the preferences of the dominant economies in the issue-area. Competition among international institutions for control over each issue-area—a diversity of arenas in which bargains could be struck or undermined—also characterized each policy area. GATT became a symbol—perhaps a misplaced one—of a deregulating or liberalizing alternative in each case. To date the changes in each regime do not support the view that economic integration points inevitably to liberalization, international pressures for deregulation, or new and stronger institutions.

Telecommunications

As Peter Cowhey described it, the "old regime" in telecommunications was the very model of a modern monopoly at both the national and international levels.[101] The International Telecommunications Union (ITU) was often portrayed as a sleepy standards-setting shop, but it served as an effective cartel for national telecommunications monopolies. In the liberal trading order overseen by GATT, the

---

101. The following account of changes in the telecommunications regime is drawn from Cowhey (1990); see also Cowhey and Aronson (1993, pp. 164–216).

telecommunications sector was treated as a government procurement issue and largely excluded from GATT scrutiny and negotiations in much the same way as agriculture.[102] The emergence of new satellite transmission technologies was accommodated within the existing regime by spinning off Intelsat, an entity whose revolutionary technology was wholly owned by the same domestic telephone companies that regulated their exchange through the ITU.

As in the financial sector, technological innovation—in this case, the digital electronics revolution—put pressure on national regulatory regimes and produced irrepressible national challenges to the old order. Those interest-driven challenges came from countries that were the biggest consumers of telecommunications services—the United States, Japan, and the United Kingdom. Technological change had created a host of new players in the sector, particularly a demanding and concentrated group of customers for telecommunications services that saw through the cartel embedded in the old ITU system. Because the United States had engaged in significant domestic deregulation that effectively opened its market in advance of other industrialized countries, it was able to use the substantial lever of market access to pry open the markets of others.

As U.S. negotiators realized, market access for telecommunications products was dependent on liberalization in markets for telecommunications services. The American agenda implied two controversial steps: moving negotiations on telecommunications to GATT, in which norms of liberalization rather than regulated monopoly held sway, and extending the reach of international surveillance over domestic regulatory structures in the sector.[103] The second portion of the strategy reflected an acute awareness of the ways in which behind-the-border regulatory regimes, superficially unrelated to trade, profoundly influenced market access.

The American strategy worked in part: telecommunications became a central part of the negotiations that produced GATS in the Uruguay Round and emphasized market access for services providers. The outcome of the Uruguay Round was more disappointing: the Annex on Telecommunications of GATS covered access to and use of public telecommunications networks, an issue of prime importance to

---

102. Cowhey and Aronson (1993, p. 168).
103. Cowhey and Aronson (1993, p. 188).

the providers of other business services such as information and financial services. Opening basic telecommunications sectors, however, remained a subject for continuing negotiations among twenty-two countries, with an end date set at April 1996. Technological change, which has driven much of the process of liberalization to date, could well outstrip the negotiators, whether they are successful or not.[104]

After the Uruguay Round, the telecommunications regime remained characterized by a "diversity of forums" for international negotiation, but GATT, favored site for the liberalizers, had assumed a far more central place in international governance of the sector. The number of countries negotiating basic telecommunications might still prove too unwieldy for detailed bargaining, leaving room for bilateral negotiations between the United States and the European Union. Such negotiations had prepared the ground for GATT negotiations but also threatened the nondiscrimination norm of GATT. Finally, the ITU itself had responded to institutional competition from GATT, although it had conceded some of its jurisdiction to the trade organization.[105]

Telecommunications reflected a central feature of GATT service negotiations: because national preferences over the degree of domestic deregulation continued to conflict, the new regime remained fragmented. Nevertheless, the externalization of domestic deregulation bargains and the expert consensus that accompanied those bargains had transformed the international regime, moving it much closer to a market access regime rather than the manager of collusive bargains between national monopolists. Available international institutions both reflected and mediated these differing views of the pace and scope of deregulation.

Banking: Regulatory Extension and Harmonization

In certain respects the pattern of international governance in the financial sector resembled that in telecommunications. Both had been highly regulated and politically sensitive parts of the national

---

104. Steinberg (1994, p. 52); Frances Williams, "Unfinished Business in Uruguay Round," *Financial Times*, August 16, 1994, p. 5.
105. Cowhey (1990, p. 193).

infrastructure. Both were the subject of often contentious bilateral negotiations between the United States, Europe, and Japan. And both were tugged into the Uruguay Round of trade negotiations as the scope of those negotiations expanded to include services. Financial services, like telecommunications, are now the subject of difficult post–Uruguay Round negotiations on market access.

Banking and financial services, however, diverged from other services sectors in two key respects that shaped the preferences of the most powerful actors over the regulatory regime. Although market access remained an issue, particularly with Japan and the developing countries, deregulation of the financial sector and its globalization posed far greater risks to national regulatory authorities and their political principals than other sectors. The financial system was a uniquely important portion of the national economic infrastructure and one that was highly sensitive (and becoming more sensitive) to shocks from international linkages. Also, the possibilities for regulatory arbitrage by private agents was far greater than in other service sectors: the ultimate consumers in telecommunications, for example, were rooted in national territories and monitored more easily. The rise of offshore financial centers with little regulatory oversight and the persistence of national banking secrecy laws expanded the possibilities for gaps in regulatory oversight that could have serious effects on the stability of national financial systems.

In addition to the familiar pattern of negotiation over market access for financial services providers, therefore, banking regulators made concerted efforts to extend and ultimately to harmonize certain elements of the international regulatory structure. At each step, these efforts to control the potential spillover effects of any lack of regulatory oversight were driven by specific financial failures or crises. The first efforts to coordinate national regulatory surveillance of the rapidly internationalizing financial sector came with the Herstatt crisis in 1974. That early warning of the risks to national banking systems was met in 1975 with the formation of the Committee on Banking Regulations and Supervisory Practices (the Basel Committee). The Basel Committee was based on the long-standing cooperative relationship among central bank governors of the G-10 at the BIS in Basel (hence its shorter title). In addition to central bank representation, each country was typically represented by another supervisory authority as well.[106] The structure of coordinated action required little additional institution-building: central bank collective action already benefited from a relatively dense set of ties and a common outlook, although preferences on the degree of regulatory oversight displayed considerable national variation.

The first measures of the committee were directed to ensuring seamless regulatory oversight in the fragmented and often opaque international financial dealings of their banks. The Concordat of 1975 was the first step in a series of agreements that assigned supervisory authority over banks operating across national borders and ensured that supervision would take place on a consolidated basis. Further amendments were made when failures or crises (particularly the Banco Ambrosiano crisis in 1982) demonstrated new gaps in the regulatory structure. Little monitoring or enforcement of the central banks by one another was built into the system: the techniques of cooperation were information sharing on the international operations of banks and consultation on new risks and regulatory dilemmas that had to be met by national regulators. Apart from coordinated understandings on the responsibilities of national regulators over the international activities of their banks, no effort was made at this point to harmonize national regulatory policies, which were simply coordinated and extended in an agreed fashion. The national regulatory patchwork became an international regulatory patchwork, but one (it was hoped) with fewer gaps.

Pressure for more explicit harmonization was interest driven and originated in the domestic political arena of the United States. The latest and greatest financial crisis—the debt crisis that opened in 1982—forced a series of delicate bargains between the Federal Reserve, which took a lead position in managing the crisis and its threats to the U.S. financial system, and Congress, which was intent on avoiding any appearance of "bailing out the banks" that were threatened by the debt implosion and imposing regulatory changes that would prevent a reccurrence of risky financial practices. The instrument chosen for these purposes was capital adequacy requirements. With the imposition of tougher requirements on American banks, however, the affected financial institutions raised competitiveness

---

106. This account of the Baesl Committee and financial regulation is based on Herring and Litan (1995); see Kapstein (1991); see also Kapstein (1992).

issues—European and Japanese rivals that did not operate under such tightened capital adequacy constraints would enjoy regulatory advantages. From the regulators' concern for safety and soundness of the financial system, the agenda was broadened to ensuring a "level playing field" for American banks against their international competitors.

This level playing field analysis was increasingly compelling in the United States during the 1980s: it was used repeatedly in trade negotiations and in the turn to "aggressive unilateralism" over unfair trading practices. In the case of banking regulations, American authorities first moved to enhance their bargaining position by forging a joint agreement with the United Kingdom on harmonizing bank capital requirements (announced January 1987). This was a clear example of preemption in a coordination game, forcing other members of the G-10 toward a new harmonized focal point under threat of denial of market access: the two major financial powers might not approve applications from international banks that did not adopt harmonized capital adequacy standards.[107]

Confronted with the Anglo-American initiative, the rest of the Basel Committee reached agreement quickly—after amendments to meet national objections—on common bank capital standards that were announced in 1988. The agreement includes only industrialized countries, but the key financial powers are all members. Whether this example of explicit harmonization of minimum standards is a harbinger of future responses to global financial integration is questionable, however. As Kapstein noted, the process was not knowledge driven: there was little expert consensus on this move toward harmonization. Although the choice of capital adequacy standards was not intellectually invalid, it was hardly the first step that would have been chosen by members of the financial and regulatory expert communities to deal with weaknesses in the international financial system.[108]

Unless additional arguments based on competitive disadvantage are pressed by the financial sectors or political actors of a major financial power, an interest-driven impetus for further harmonization also appears weak. Also, there are institutional obstacles to extending

107. On the political dimensions of the move toward harmonized standards, see Kapstein (1991, pp. 12–20).
108. Kapstein (1992, pp. 286–87).

the harmonization of national regulations in the face of global financial integration. As a recent evaluation of the 1988 Capital Accord demonstrates, harmonization of national policies on a single dimension is unlikely to erase other, more significant features of the competitive playing field.[109] Harmonization negotiations then become exercises in peeling a large onion: accounting rules, legal regimes, capital markets, and other domestic differences all have significant effects on the outcomes of the first exercise in harmonization. The pursuit of the level playing field leads down countless additional avenues. As Herring and Litan noted, even if additional harmonization can be negotiated, the ability of Basel Committee coordinating mechanisms to monitor and enforce such agreements is doubtful. The Basel Committee faces the same dilemmas confronted by GATT and other international institutions in dealing with economic integration and behind-the-border regulatory differences: developing means to extend surveillance into domestic regulatory structures that have not been subject to such scrutiny in the past. Because preferences among central banks and regulators have been aligned in favor of extending their regulatory reach internationally, the incentives to defect from the earlier coordination bargains were slight. National regulatory regimes in the financial sector are much more deeply embedded in political bargains, however, and internationally agreed changes are much more prone to pressures undermining their implementation.

Global financial integration renders renewed efforts at explicit harmonization less possible and less necessary. Private financial institutions are not engaged solely in a search for the least regulated environment: as Herring and Litan pointed out, the pressures for a "race to the bottom" may be less powerful than many believe. The market will often reinforce the judgments of regulatory authorities on such issues as capital adequacy. In any case, the rate of innovation in financial markets is so great that carefully negotiated bargains to harmonize national regulations are likely to lag behind the market; better, in this view, to pursue the original and more efficient path of information exchange so that a more decentralized process of coordinating national regulation is accomplished more effectively.[110]

109. Scott and Iwahara (1994).
110. Herring and Litan (1995); see also Kapstein (1992).

Environmental Regulation and the Pressures of Integration

As GATT became the preferred site for multilateral negotiations to ensure market access, its negotiations increasingly targeted domestic regulatory regimes. Those seeking market access under GATT auspices have had to confront deeply entrenched regulatory regimes and their international reflections, based on regulated industries and the domestic regulatory agencies that oversee them (or have been captured by them). Environmental protection and regulation, however, presents a different set of political players: a regulatory apparatus of relatively recent formation, one with close connections to the scientific community in many instances, and above all, one with varying degrees of domestic support among nongovernmental organizations and political activists. Despite these differences with regulatory regimes based on economic interests, the new pattern of environmental regulation could also be seen as threatened by the liberalizing norms of GATT. The possibilities for friction between the two regimes were apparent. In the 1990s that potential exploded into open confrontation between sections of the environmental movement and GATT, spilling over into opposition to the North American Free Trade Agreement (NAFTA) (see chapter 3).

Much of the conflict was knowledge driven. In this instance, the concept of epistemic community does seem useful: the debate between trade liberalizers and environmentalists often seemed a dialogue of the deaf. GATT and the academics (principally economists) who dealt with trade issues had few organizational or intellectual connections to the environmentalists; the ignorance of trade issues and policymaking on the side of environmentalists was equally profound. The two intellectual universes had moved with their own logic and research agendas; few bridges had been constructed before friction became open conflict.

Equally important were the institutional underpinnings of conflict between environmentalists and GATT. In the eyes of many environmentalists, international environmental regimes were weak, decentralized, and lacking enforcement mechanisms. There was no centralized global environmental regime comparable to GATT or the IMF; the patchwork of regimes that had evolved to deal with environmental issues—from protecting the ozone layer to protecting endangered species—was characterized by lack of clarity in its rules and no clear means of coordination. In short, many in the environmental community appeared to share the legalist diagnosis of institutional shortcomings, despite evidence that centralized enforcement was not crucial to the success of environmental regimes.[111] The institutional connection to trade was clear: trade instruments—the threat of closing markets to environmental violators—were increasingly incorporated in national environmental legislation that attempted to extend environmental regulation beyond national boundaries.

A second anxiety concerned both international environmental institutions and domestic environmental regimes: increasing economic integration would permit regulatory arbitrage through "environmental dumping." Firms and countries would benefit economically through lower regulatory standards, undermining international regimes (which they might refuse to join) and placing pressure on the environmental standards of other, more heavily regulated ("greener") states. Worse, norms of liberalization might forbid discrimination against the products from such settings on the grounds that environmental regulations of this sort were simply disguised protectionism.

Environmentalist anxieties at a time of growing activism were heightened by a GATT panel decision that guaranteed immediate and intense scrutiny of the links between global regimes that embodied a norm of liberalization, such as GATT, and regulatory regimes to protect the environment, health, and consumer safety. In 1991 a GATT dispute settlement panel found an American ban on imports of Mexican tuna under the Marine Mammal Protection Act (MMPA) to be in contravention of GATT obligations.[112] Interpretations of the panel decision remain divided. Some experts held that the core of the panel finding concerned nondiscrimination and that the implications for other environmental regulation under GATT were overblown: unlike the European Community ban on particular techniques of fur trapping, the United States had not forbidden a particular technique of fishing for *both* its own nationals and others.[113] The points seized on by environmentalists, however, concerned both of the threats described above. The panel rejected the extrajurisdictional application

111. See the analysis of Petersmann (1993, pp. 44–47). For a contrary view on enforcement, see Haas, Keohane, and Levy (1993, p. 398).

112. For a summary and analysis of the case and the panel report, see Trachtman (1992).

113. Palmeter (1993, pp. 65–66).

of the exceptions in article XX (b and g) of the General Agreement: a distinction was made between protecting the domestic environment and attempting to extend national environmental standards unilaterally to the regulatory regimes of other countries—harmonization through the threat of denying market access. The panel rejected the U.S. interpretation on this point, since it would "allow each country to sit in judgment of the internal regulatory scheme of each other country, restricting the flexibility of each country to establish its own standards."[114] It was this part of the ruling that most alarmed American environmentalists. The panel also found against the United States on the issue of regulating the production processes of a product rather than the product itself. On another reading, it was not clear that process standards were prohibited if they did not have protectionist effects and did not discriminate.[115] Because discrimination between goods from "dirty" sources as opposed to goods produced in a "green" manner is one instrument of environmental regulation, environmentalists were concerned that GATT might prevent such distinctions according to mode of production.

The issue of a potential threat to *domestic* environmental regulations from GATT was not part of the 1991 panel report, but the attention given to "environmental dumping" in the heated debate over NAFTA contributed to closer examination of Uruguay Round negotiations by environmentalists. The Technical Barriers Agreement and the Agreement on Sanitary and Phytosanitary Measures were objectionable to some environmentalists, because they appeared less "green" (protective of environmental standards) than NAFTA. In particular, the "least trade restrictive" standard would permit challenge to claimed exceptions (under article XX) for environmental purposes. Trade specialists found little evidence in the history of GATT for successful challenges that would tend to undermine national environmental regulations through a regulatory "race to the bottom." So long as the regulation or standard in question was nondiscriminatory, the record of GATT decisions suggested that a challenge would be "uphill, steeply uphill."[116]

---

114. Trachtman (1993, p. 149).
115. Petersmann (1993, p. 68).
116. For the environmentalist view, see Charnovitz (1993, p. 51); for a trade policy view, see Palmeter (1993, p. 68).

Political attacks on GATT norms and rules were met first with warnings from GATT that environmental concerns should not be captured by protectionists and that unilateral efforts to extend national practices through trade measures would result in endless conflict. More constructively and classically for the ever-adaptable GATT, the trade organization reactivated the Group on Environmental Measures and International Trade in November 1991 after twenty years of dormancy. (The Committee on Trade and Development also took up part of the GATT agenda on the environment.) One set of issues that was immediately considered concerned "eco-labeling" and its effects on trade. In general, the GATT group emphasized transparency in packaging and labeling requirements that might have substantial trade effects. More attention was focused on an issue that posed real risks of conflict between GATT rules and environmental agreements: the use of trade provisions as a means of enforcement in multilateral environmental agreements (MEAs). (The MMPA was a unilateral American policy that did not have endorsement in multilateral agreements.) Discussion in the Group on Environmental Measures and International Trade to date has suggested two ways to deal with this issue: through a collective interpretation of article XX that provided a general exception to agreements that reflect "genuinely multilateral consensus" or through a case-by-case granting of individual waivers under article XXV. Because any MEA that enjoyed wide support would also enjoy the support of most members of GATT, conflict would probably be rare. More difficult, however, would be the application of trade measures to discourage free riding by nonmembers of an environmental agreement (who might be members of GATT). Some members believe that some ex ante criteria for environmental agreements need to be established so that they can be negotiated in a GATT-compatible manner.[117]

Trade policy specialists who turned their attention to the links between trade and the environment have agreed that, on closer examination, the actual areas of conflict between trade and the environment range from "the nonexistent" to "the minimal."[118] Trade

---

117. For an excellent summary of the arguments for different strategies in dealing with this potential conflict, see "GATT Council to Review UNCED Follow-Up after the Conclusion of the Round," *Trade and the Environment*, November 26, 1994, pp. 4–6.

118. Palmeter (1993, p. 55).

instruments are not well designed to serve environmental purposes, and above all, liberalized trade is not a source of environmental problems in and of itself.[119] In general, much of the apparent conflict between trade and environmental policy communities is knowledge driven. Issues such as "environmental dumping" and "pollution havens" have seldom been carefully investigated, and the evidence that exists suggests those fears are overdrawn.[120] Little evidence is presented for a regulatory race to the bottom in environmental protection.

Knowledge-driven divisions run deeper than the lack of scientific evidence, however. One key belief, strongly held by trade analysts (and economists more broadly), seems unlikely to win easy converts among environmental activists: that a higher volume of trade and higher economic growth will produce beneficial environmental effects, through more efficient resource allocation and through demands for greater environmental protection by more affluent populations. For those intent on sustainable economic development, such arguments are yet another example of "trickle-down" propositions that work only in the long run. Similar arguments are made regarding the unilateral use of trade instruments to enforce harmonization of environmental standards upward. Although specific spillovers affecting other societies may not be present, environmentalists often respond to psychological externalities, much as human rights activists do—a demonstrable economic "bad" affecting other societies is not required. The politics of psychological externalities may be difficult to deal with in an organization such as GATT, which is founded on utilitarian calculation and bargaining.

As important as these knowledge-driven divisions with the trade policy community are, there are also two political logics at work. International environmental regimes—when international consensus can be reached—appear toothless: trade instruments are necessary means of enforcement for many environmentalists. In the absence of multilateral consensus, wielding market access in a unilateral fashion may accelerate harmonization of national environmental regulations. At the same time, harmonization downward through deregulation may result, not only from formal challenges under GATT but from

---

119. Anderson and Blackhurst (1992, pp. 20–21). Similiar conclusions are reached by Sorsa (1992).
120. Birdsall and Wheeler (1993).

the political balance that is created internally under conditions of greater external liberalization. Those urging tougher regulation in the interests of environmental protection see their political power undermined by arguments over international competitiveness that include an implicit threat of exit by firms from "over-regulated" economies. It is not clear whether a better demonstration of the causal links between environmental protection and trade liberalization will overcome these concerns.

Global Economic Institutions and Economic Integration

Even after this limited survey of global economic institutions, the patterns that emerge call into question any simple relationship among economic integration, the national strategies deployed to deal with the tension between international integration and continued political segmentation, and the evolution of international institutions. Economic integration, driven by technological innovation and national policy choices, has not produced a consistent pattern in choice of strategy (harmonization versus mutual recognition, for example) or in the timing of efforts to deal with the effects of economic integration. Instead, in most of the cases examined, the significance of these issues on the international agenda and the urgency with which they are pressed are best explained by shifts in knowledge that change the interpretations of key national actors or by economic interests that foresee economic gain or disadvantage from the extension of economic exchange and market integration. The politics of interpreting change is often linked to the mobilization of interests. The connection of competitive disadvantage to capital standards in banking, the trade and the environment debate, and the eventual acceptance of services as part of GATT negotiations all illustrate that knowledge- and interest-driven processes are difficult to separate.

Institutional outcomes also fail to demonstrate any clear trend toward stronger, more centralized, or rule-based institutions. The contrasting histories of GATT and the IMF suggest that economic integration of particular kinds may undermine existing "strong" institutions. Even GATT, which does appear as a more centralized institution with stronger powers of monitoring and enforcement (although the means of enforcement remain decentralized), may in fact owe its institutional recuperation and its wider scope to other "strengths": its decentralized, adaptable, and open architecture and a set of core principles that have achieved wide acceptance for achieving market access. The pattern that best captures this institutional array is policed or monitored decentralization, permitting considerable latitude for national autonomy within broad bands of policy harmonization. The broad framework of GATS and the TRIPS Agreement, the post-1985 policy coordination regime, and the pattern of international banking coordination (before the explicit harmonization of the 1988 Basel Accord) all fit such a pattern.

The record of global economic institutions also reflects persistent dilemmas in institutional design. Because these are global institutions, they must satisfy both their industrialized and more powerful members, willing to pursue new agenda items in plurilateral settings, and the need to maintain their global status by engaging the developing and transitional economies. As concern over free riding by smaller members of the regime has grown, this dilemma has deepened. Decisionmaking efficiency may also decline as institutional scope widens, yet wider scope has permitted institutions such as GATT to effect valuable bargains through cross-issue linkage. Without such cross-issue bargaining, it is unlikely that the Uruguay Round could even have begun.

Most of these institutions, particularly the IMF and GATT, have lacked strong direct links to domestic interests, whether knowledge- or interest-based. They have avoided capture by such interests and the conservatism and decline that may result (the fate of the ITU may be a case in point), but they have also forgone important sources of information and residual political support. Both GATT and the IMF, given their histories as institutions beholden to their governmental shareholders, have found it difficult to deal with demands from new stakeholders—nongovernmental organizations, in particular—and to incorporate such claimants into their decisionmaking.

The respective histories of GATT and the IMF demonstrate the fragility of rule-based institutions in the face of unexpected shocks and rapid international economic change. Whether the IMF possessed significant influence over national policies, even in the heyday of Bretton Woods, remains a controversial point. With the end of the par value system, however, the IMF was unable to reconstruct a new role for itself at the center of a more informal, ad hoc system of policy coordination. Even the renovated GATT system of dispute settlement retains a strong element of mediation and conciliation through negotiation. The innovations in global regulatory regimes, particularly the modest efforts at explicit harmonization of capital standards, do not suggest that rule-based institutions will necessarily become more common as economic integration advances. Instead, the shortcomings of such institutions, wedded to specific environments, have produced a bias toward more decentralized, open, and adaptable structures that will not be left in a backwash of irrelevance by international economic change.

Finally, each of these institutions, in pursuing its oversight or surveillance of national policies, has had to devise new means to encourage greater transparency in previously "domestic" practices, to monitor national regulatory policies, and to incorporate and interpret a changing body of information (in the case of financial markets, rapidly changing) about the international economy. In each case, the frontier of conflict runs along a divide between national policies that were not previously subject to international surveillance and international demands for intensified scrutiny of and agreed change in those policies because of unrecognized externalities.

Each of these dilemmas is clarified at the regional level, where institutional experimentation and innovation has taken place in a bargaining context of smaller numbers and high levels of economic integration. Those institutions are discussed next.

Chapter 3

Variation in Regional Institutions

REGIONAL institution building demonstrates a cyclical pattern that belies any simple explanation based on the demands of economic integration. Interest in new regional initiatives has risen and fallen according to a political tempo, and the pace of evolution among established regional institutions has fluctuated over time. In western Europe, for example, the institutional stagnation of the early 1980s was transmuted into Euro-optimism after the Single European Act and the Maastricht Treaty. That burst of forward motion slowed in turn after the Danish and French referenda and the crisis of the European exchange rate mechanism in 1992–93.

The first wave of regional institutions appeared in the late 1950s and early 1960s, in part as an imitation of the newly established European Common Market. The extent of the move toward regional economic arrangements rivaled that of the 1990s: by the mid-1960s, more than half of the contracting parties to the General Agreement on Tariffs and Trade (GATT) were part of a regional bloc or bloc-in-formation.[1] The motivations for this burst of activity, however, were sharply divergent in industrialized groupings such as the European Community and among developing countries. In the latter group, the logic was that of the Economic Commission for Latin America: development of a market large enough for import substitution, a goal that implied little if any external liberalization and only very cautious intraregional removal of barriers to exchange. These developing country free-trade areas typically lacked strong institu-

---

1. Patterson (1966, pp. 140–41).

tions in the form of effective dispute settlement mechanisms, enforcement provisions, or capacity to compensate those disadvantaged by economic opening. The accomplishments of these early regional experiments in the south were limited. Plagued by political conflicts and erratic macroeconomic policies, supported by only weak coalitions of interests in support of across-the-board liberalization, few significant economic gains were realized. Although many survived into the 1980s, by and large regionalism of the first generation was transformed into joint cooperative activities of very limited scope.[2]

A second wave of regional institution building that began in the late 1980s was, like the first, driven in part by a new burst of consolidation in the European Community, producing first the Single European Act and then the Maastricht Treaty to form a European Union (EU). The intensification of institutional development in western Europe had a "billiard ball" effect on the rest of the world, heightening concerns that the GATT regime was fragmenting, forcing decisions for membership on many of the EC's smaller neighbors, and causing other countries to consider regional insurance against erosion at the global level.

Despite the European stimulus that they shared with earlier periods, these new regional initiatives, which were both revivals of dormant arrangements (such as the Central American Common Market and the Andean Pact) and entirely new creations (such as the North American Free Trade Agreement [NAFTA] and Asia-Pacific Economic Cooperation [APEC]), differed markedly from the earlier wave of regional experimentation in two respects. First, the overriding substantive content of the new arrangements was liberalizing, despite discriminatory features. Liberalization was often programmed in an across-the-board fashion rather than using a painstaking sectoral incrementalism. Second, arrangements that included industrialized and developing countries under the same institutional roof, which had been rare, appeared more frequently. The concessions made in such agreements were increasingly reciprocal in nature. The goals of the two types of partners converged on the joint gains to be made from shallow integration—removal of the many barriers to exchange that remained at the border. Beyond those goals, industrialized and

2. On this first wave of regionalist experiments, de la Torre and Kelly (1992, pp. 25–37); Langhammer and Hiemenz (1990, pp. 57–60).

industrializing countries advanced different agendas. For the industrialized countries, particularly the United States, regional arrangements provided a means for dealing with a "GATT-plus" agenda, which included issues of deeper integration, behind-the-border issues such as investment regimes, regulation of services, and environmental and labor standards. For developing countries, the arrangements promised to constrain or at least render more predictable the use of trade policy instruments in industrialized markets as well as adding a valuable increment of credibility to their new programs of liberalization, binding successor governments to a path of opening to the international economy.

In contrast to the EU, these new and revived free-trade areas are seldom "supported by significant supranational institutions or elaborate mechanisms for common decisionmaking."[3] Substantial variation in institutional design across regions and innovation in areas such as dispute settlement offers one way to test the implications of intensified economic integration for divergent national policies and international institutions. In explaining and assessing that pattern of variation, the EU's evolving institutions provide an important benchmark for other regional institutional arrangements. Despite its virtually unique institutions, the EU continues to confront many of the same dilemmas that other, less institutionalized arrangements face.

European Union: The Institutional Logic of Deeper Integration

Looking back on more than three decades of European institutional evolution, the process may appear as two interrelated and linear trends: economic integration proceeding in tandem with stronger institutions. In fact, institution building in Europe has followed a jagged trajectory, although growing economic interdependence and an investment by interest groups in a more predictable European environment has underlain it. Charles de Gaulle temporarily halted an initial period of rapid institutional strengthening in the mid-1960s; international economic turmoil disrupted ambitious institutional initiatives in the 1970s. Euro-stagnation in the early 1980s, which appeared

3. De la Torre and Kelly (1992, p. 13).

terminal to some, was rapidly transformed into a surprising renewal of movement toward completion of the internal market under the Single European Act and a further strengthening of institutions and widening of scope in the creation of the EU at the Maastricht Summit in 1991.

Defining the European Edifice: Models of Institutional Development

The stop-and-go pattern of European institution building suggests two broad political dynamics at work. Internally, politicians have used European Community institutions to solve knotty political problems that can be managed at the national level only inefficiently or at great cost. This dynamic incorporates those issues that result directly from policy spillovers in the course of economic integration, but the problem-solving dynamic is broader than a simple economic spillover model would imply. An international dynamic has been at work as well. Even though European initiatives toward integration have shaped the international environment and spurred regional responses in other parts of the world, Europe has itself been shaped by perceptions of the international political and economic environment. The Soviet threat and the U.S. support that it inspired were crucial in the early years of the European Common Market; more recently, perceived international economic disorder (such as the fraying of the Bretton Woods monetary regime) and competitive threats from economic rivals (first the United States and then Japan) have served as an impetus to further internal liberalization and institution building.

The result has been an institutional edifice that is difficult to define in conventional terms. Two broad views of the European institutional nexus point toward different responses to further economic integration. Stanley Hoffmann and Robert O. Keohane presented a point of view best described as "regime-plus." The EU evidences a higher level of commitment from its members than most international institutions; it is also "more centralized and institutionalized." Its distinctiveness in this view lies not in its "statelike" or "prefederal" characteristics but in the pooling of sovereignty through an incremental process. This process has produced over time a "network form of organization" that is not captured in an adversarial image of states versus European institutions.[4] The alternative federalist image of the

4. Hoffmann and Keohane (1991, pp. 7, 10).

European project is familiar within European integrationist circles, but the EU remains a "federal system–minus." As Alberta Sbragia pointed out, the national governments that make up the EU have far more influence than the constituent states of any existing federal system.[5] The level of commonality in economic space does approach and even surpass federal states, however, and comparisons with federal systems also serve to illuminate the choices between centralized and decentralized modalities in dealing with deeper integration issues (harmonization versus mutual recognition; subsidiarity versus Euronorms).

Institutional developments of the past decade demonstrate the slippery quality of European institutional evolution. Proto-federalists point to evidence of strengthening, such as new enforcement powers for the European Court and an enlarged role for the European Parliament. The EU has also widened the scope of future common policies. The Maastricht Treaty included a plan for economic and monetary union (a common currency and a European central bank) and two new "pillars": justice and home affairs and a common foreign and security policy. Skeptics who endorse a regime-plus paradigm can point to the continued requirement of consensus for fundamental decisions within the EU (a Charles de Gaulle could still bring EU business to a halt), the near-failure of the European monetary system (EMS) in 1992–93, and the small scale of EU resources, when compared to those of national governments.[6] Also, renewed institution building has been paralleled by calls for emphasis on subsidiarity and mutual recognition, decentralized solutions that appear to run counter to the older centralized model of harmonization to common European standards. The attachments of European citizens are also lower than would be expected in a federal arrangement: the referenda held after the Maastricht Agreement indicated how thin support for European integration had become in some member states. Popular support for European integration has long displayed wide variation cross-nationally and a close relationship to economic conditions. Euro-barometer polls have revealed a surprisingly weak level of popular support for the European project during the recent European recession.[7]

5. Sbragia (1992, p. 5).
6. A survey of these recent developments is given in Corbett (1992, pp. 297–98).
7. See, for example, "Europeans? Us?" *The Economist*, December 11, 1993, p. 54. On cross-national variation and the economic link, see Eichenberg and Dalton (1993).

The characteristics of European institutions that place them apart from other regional enterprises in the 1990s are neither their statelike qualities nor their strength vis-à-vis member governments. The nomenclature of EU institutions (Parliament, Court) may obscure as much as it clarifies about the defining features of EU institutions. The three institutional dimensions that set the EU apart from other regional groups lie instead in the degree of institutional delegation incorporated in the evolving European "constitution," the scope of European bargains, and perhaps most important, the domestic political linkages constructed between European and national institutions. If there is a "European model" for the future of other regional arrangements, it lies in these characteristics.

First, the member states of the EU have delegated more important and extensive functions to European institutions than has been the case with the members of other international or regional institutions. The Commission, for example, surpasses even the strong secretariat of an international organization. Its initiating role, awarded in the Treaty of Rome, and its enforcement role, however nonconfrontational in practice, have few parallels among other international groupings. The degree of delegation to European institutions has made it nearly impossible to exclude those institutions from the regularized network of intergovernmental bargaining that determines European policies. Although periodic efforts are made to restrain and circumscribe the behavioral ambit of European institutions (such as the containment efforts directed at the European Court in the Maastricht Agreement), interstate bargaining must at least anticipate the likely reactions of the European Court, the Commission, and increasingly, the Parliament. To understand this key distinction between European and global institutions, a comparison with the International Monetary Fund (IMF) is useful: its participation in the G-5/G-7 policy coordination process after the breakdown of the Bretton Woods exchange rate regime was only at the sufferance of the major monetary powers. Such exclusion of core European institutions and their representatives is difficult to imagine in the European context.

Equally important is the way in which the EU has expanded its scope across issue-areas. Instead of simply adding new policy competences in a disconnected fashion, an increasingly dense network of interdependent bargains has been constructed. Third-party enforcement by institutions such as the Commission or the Court has been far less important in deepening compliance with European directives and law than national reputational considerations linked to this web of commitments, considerations that serve as a central binding device within the EU. With each new set of bargains—most recently in the expansion of scope at Maastricht—the strength of the EU increases. At critical points in European institutional development—such as the crisis in the EMS induced by Mitterrand's France in 1982–83—the effects of reneging in one sphere on valuable bargains in another have served to keep European institutions intact. One can push this argument further and suggest, as John Ruggie has done, that the EU as an entity—not simply its "central institutional apparatus"—has become an integral part of national self-definition and identity. The EU is not "out there" but is becoming part of the internal and "national" political process.[8]

Such absorption of a European dimension into national decision-making is confirmed by a final dimension in the apparent strength of European institutions: their linkages to the domestic political institutions and interests within member states, connections that are far more substantial and intricate than those of any other international institution. Those links, far more than the capabilities of European institutions alone for monitoring and enforcement, provide a basis for ensuring that European bargains are implemented. European institutions face the same obstacles to monitoring and sanctioning national behavior that other international institutions have confronted, obstacles that have only grown more formidable with deeper integration. Unlike other international institutions, however, European institutions have deployed their domestic (national) allies to at least partially overcome those obstacles.

The European Court of Justice is the most striking example of an alignment with domestic institutions that was not foreseen by the founders of the European Community. The place of European law in cementing the European institutional frame has long been recognized as virtually unique among international institutions. No other international organization "enjoys such reliably effective supremacy of its law over the laws of member governments, with a recognized Court of Justice to adjudicate disputes."[9] Less familiar is the uncertainty sur-

8. Ruggie (1993b, p. 172).
9. Hoffmann and Keohane (1991, p. 11).

rounding the sources of this supremacy. The preeminence of EC law is hardly clear cut in the Treaty of Rome; its de facto status has been constructed through the actions of national courts. Lower courts in particular have regularly invoked article 177 of the Treaty of Rome, elevating the status of the European Court to the detriment of their own higher courts.[10] This collaboration by national courts is essential for the effectiveness of the European Court, not only because of ambiguity in the status of European law, but because litigants themselves do not have locus standi to appeal under article 177 and because, until the Maastricht Agreement, the European Court lacked the sanctions to enforce its judgments.[11]

This peculiar transnational alliance is based on a mutual interest in the empowerment of the lower courts by granting them effective oversight over national legislation and the desire of private litigants and their lawyers to call on European Community law in national courts.[12] In their analysis of the *Cassis de Dijon* decision, often taken as a demonstration of the European Court's power, Karen Alter and Sophie Meunier-Aitsahalia proposed another more indirect and political process through which judicial decisions influence national politics and European policy. In this view, it is not linkages to national court systems that are always of primary importance. Rather, the Court provides access to interest groups and firms that wish to break up collusive bargains reached at the Community level and serves to provoke a political response at the national level, one that may use a European Court judgment as a focal point.[13]

If the "judicial creativity" of the European Court and the national courts has forged an unusually durable link between European and domestic institutions, other parts of the European policy process demonstrate similar interweaving. The administrative processes of member governments have become more closely connected to Brussels, undermining any view that simply pits "Europe" against national prerogatives. Monitoring of national implementation of European agreements is rendered less difficult (and less essential) by the intensive negotiation that occurs among European and national bureau-

10. Shapiro (1992, p. 127).
11. See Mancini (1991, pp. 180–84).
12. For a neofunctionalist argument that emphasizes the national interests in these links, see Burley and Mattli (1993).
13. Alter and Meunier-Aitsahalia (1994).

cratic players as European policies are developed. This phenomenon has been labeled "bureaucratic intermingling" (Ludlow) or "comitology" (Williams), the involvement well below the ministerial level of national civil servants in the European policy process.[14] Others have noted the exclusion of certain other political players from the emerging "iron triangles" of Europe-wide interest groups, European and national administrations, and to a degree, European parliamentary committees; the "losers" are national politicians and parliaments.[15]

This "democratic deficit" suggests a final link to national politics, the European Parliament, uniformly regarded as the weakest of those links. Although the European Parliament has been directly elected since 1979, its powers have been limited: a largely unusable power to dismiss the Commission, a power of assent to new members and trade and cooperation agreements, and after the Single European Act, an enhancement of its legislative oversight in certain categories. It has not had authority to raise revenue, however, and its ability to scrutinize implementation and initiate policy has been marginal.[16] In part, the Parliament's inability to insert itself into the European political process rests on its lack of domestic anchorages of the sort that the Court, the council, and the Commission enjoy. The electoral and party connections have proved too slender to support an enlarged role. The Maastricht Treaty did enhance the role of the Parliament, requiring from 1995 a vote of confidence in a new Commission and "consultation" over the choice of president of the Commission. The treaty also widened the ability of the Parliament to scrutinize European legislation and administration.[17] Nevertheless, legislative initiation remained a Commission monopoly, and although the Parliament gained veto power over certain legislative categories, the council retained its right to act unilaterally in the absence of such a veto.[18] The direct connection to electorates represented by the European Parlia-

14. Ludlow (1991, p. 103); Williams (1991, p. 158).
15. Wessels (1991a); Wessels (1991b, pp. 140–41).
16. Williams (1991, pp. 160–61).
17. An indicator of its increased confidence was the narrow vote approving Jacques Santer to succeed Jacques Delors as president of the Commission in July 1994.
18. For a complete review of changes in the Parliament's powers in the Maastricht Treaty, see Corbett (1992).

ment is unique among international institutions; the Maastricht negotiations are only the latest demonstration that member states remain wary of this link.

The emphasis in some treatments of the EU on its abilities to enforce compliance to supranational norms or directives has been overstated as a measure of its strength and of the degree of national compliance. Although the Commission has a prominent role in initiating European legislation, its monitoring and enforcement role has been limited: in any effort at enforcement, "emphasis was placed on cooperation and agreement rather than confrontation."[19] The Commission devoted much less attention to this dimension of its responsibilities than it did to policy formulation. As Ludlow argued, the portrait of Commission action that emerges from auditors' reports is "more often than not . . . timid in its demands, unclear in its instructions, and amateurish in its surveillance."[20] These shortcomings appear less grave, however, if one abandons a simple view of European institutional strength as measured in formal institutions and centralization. The alternative domestic links forged by European institutions provided a different, and arguably more effective, means to ensure compliance than an image of monitoring and enforcement from the "outside."

Institutional Dilemmas in the EU

The EU is unusual among regional groups for the density and scope of its interdependent bargains, for the extensive delegation of active roles to European institutions, and above all, for its carefully constructed links to national polities. On other dimensions, it reveals dilemmas that closely resemble those of other regional and global institutions.

CENTRALIZATION VERSUS DECENTRALIZATION: THE BOUNDARIES OF SUBSIDIARITY. Since the *Cassis de Dijon* decision of the European Court and the ratification of the Single European Act, considerable attention has been given to the benefits and costs of mutual recognition of national standards and policies as weighed against harmonization to negotiated European standards. The inadequacies of an

19. Ludlow (1991, p. 104).
20. Ludlow (1991, p. 108).

explicit harmonization approach were clearly documented in the European Community before adoption of the Single European Act. The requirement of unanimity in European Community decisionmaking partly explained the painfully slow and cumbersome process of achieving agreement on harmonized standards. Decisionmaking inefficiency permitted proliferation of new regulations at the national level that outstripped the pace of European harmonization as well as technological innovation that rendered "Euro-standards" obsolete. Also, the pace of harmonization was slowed by straining for excessive uniformity in national regulations and standards and by the implementation bottlenecks that resulted from transforming EC directives under article 100 into national legal provisions.[21] Once again, even in the highly institutionalized environment of the European Community, monitoring of national implementation proved difficult. Direct regulatory power over private agents continued to rest with national governments, creating obstacles to European policymaking that were shared with other international institutions.[22]

These dilemmas produced by a centralized model of harmonization were circumvented in part by the new model of standardization introduced by the Single European Act. Although mutual recognition of national standards and regulations is often placed in opposition to an explicit harmonization approach, the turn to mutual recognition has typically taken place within widened bands of harmonization established by "fundamental requirements" in European Community directives.

Both harmonization and mutual recognition in the EU have been directed largely toward the removal of barriers to the movement of goods and capital. The development of more positive regulatory policies in areas such as the environment and labor has been slower to emerge: proponents of strong policy regimes in such areas turned in the past to national governments. As the decentralized mutual recognition model of regulatory competition takes hold in the EU, however, the perceived security of "high regulation" national regimes is at risk through regulatory competition. As a result, a pattern resembling that of federal systems such as the United States may begin to emerge.

21. Pelkmans (1987, pp. 252–53); Dehousse (1992, pp. 391–92).
22. Dehousse (1992, p. 392).

Previously, barriers to intra-EC exchange served to shelter national regulatory regimes from competitive pressures. As those shelters are stripped away, high-regulation states confront a different game: attempting to opt out of European regulatory standards, thereby disadvantaging their producers, or shifting the regulatory regime to the center—harmonizing upward. As Dehousse pointed out, the proponents of state intervention on behalf of social goals such as environmental protection and labor standards are already demonstrating their awareness of the changed and more decentralized game introduced by the Single European Act.[23] Greater decentralization may in the long run produce another cycle of policy transfer to European institutions as those demanding regulatory protection shift their attention from the national arena to Brussels.

Debate over the Social Charter demonstrates this political dynamic most clearly: those who fear relative losses in the redistribution induced by further economic integration demand further harmonization at the level of the European Community. As the implications of the new moves toward removing market barriers became clear in the late 1980s, the perceived threat to those systems of industrial relations that were more regulated and protected became politically potent, whatever the realities of "social dumping."[24] Labor unions, supported by some governments and employers, demanded harmonization of labor standards to European standards so that their own practices would be in less danger from competitive pressures. The Social Charter adopted at Maastricht displayed "impressive ambiguity" because of conflicting political pressures, and the United Kingdom was finally permitted to opt out of this European agreement. The charter provided for delegation to the social partners of authority to negotiate broad agreement on certain social issues, and qualified majority voting was also agreed on some issues. Impasse persisted on others, however, in particular, worker participation in management.[25] Depending on the strategic choices of labor and other key political actors, three futures are possible: a degree of harmonization, driven

23. Dehousse (1992, p. 397).
24. For a skeptical view on the threat from social dumping, see Center for Economic Policy Research (1993, pp. 101–15).
25. Reder and Ulman (1993, pp. 40–41); Lange (1992).

by political concerns rather than any clear evidence of a regulatory "race to the bottom," persistence of national patterns as fears of competitive deregulation evaporate and national differences reemerge in the labor movement, or even Community-wide unionism, as unions imitate the Europeanization of corporations (a trend that is virtually invisible today).[26]

The Maastricht Treaty introduced the concept of subsidiarity—the appropriate allocation of policy responsibility among the European, national, and subnational levels of government—into debate over the future of the EU. After Maastricht, national criticism of centralized models of the European future served to confirm the importance of subsidiarity. Unfortunately, as a recent study pointed out, the principles governing this key question within the EU have been "surprisingly unclear and informal, and they do not appear to rest upon a compelling economic or legal logic."[27] One key tension is that between the efficiency and credibility advantages of centralized policies at the European level (at least in those areas in which spillovers are pronounced) on the one hand and the desirability of more accountable policies, implying a greater measure of devaluation, on the other. A survey of the present distribution of competences between the European and national levels suggests that certain European policies cannot be justified on the basis of these normative criteria. (Neither a Common Agricultural Policy nor a Social Charter can be defended, for example.)[28] The poor fit between principles of subisidiarity defined in this way and the actual pattern of European policy lend further support to a political model of European institution building.

WIDENING AND DEEPENING: THE ISSUE OF NUMBER. The EU, in part because of its perceived success and the benefits that accrue to membership, resembles other regional and plurilateral institutions in weighing the benefits of further enlargement against the possible costs that such enlargement might impose on decisionmaking efficiency and further institution building. This dilemma is sometimes

26. On the likelihood of these options, see Lange (1992); Streeck (1993); Reder and Ulman (1993, pp. 38–39).
27. Center for Economic Policy Research (1993, p. 13).
28. Center for Economic Policy Research (1993).

denied, but larger numbers under existing rules represent a threat of institutional stalemate. Optimistic observers remark that preceding enlargements produced institutional innovations—in particular, increasing the scope of qualified majority voting under the Single European Act—that ultimately enhanced decisionmaking efficiency because of this threat.[29] Nevertheless, the strenuous objections raised by the United Kingdom during negotiations for the accession of the European Free Trade Association (EFTA) applicants (Austria, Finland, Sweden, and Norway) suggest the difficulties in adjusting internal decisionmaking rules, even to accommodate members that closely resemble the existing club. The European Union could restrict the issues that require unanimity, following the precedent of the Single European Act; change the formulas for "qualified majorities" (the most contentious issue during the EFTA negotiations); and redesign the voting weights of the member states. Changes in the size and formulas for representation on the Commission will be necessary if that central institution (soon to reach more than twenty in size) is to remain a capable instrument for the EU.[30]

Changing institutional rules to accommodate more members that closely resemble the existing membership is a relatively easy task, however. Widening also implies more heterogeneous preferences over European policies and the future course of European integration. To deal with such heterogeneity, a second strategy was broached at Maastricht: creating a "multispeed" EU. This approach to divergent views over the appropriate scope of the future EU was apparent in the decision to permit the United Kingdom to opt out of the Social Charter and in the provisions for a future Economic and Monetary Union, which included special arrangements for Denmark and the United Kingdom and established criteria for adherence that might be met by as few as seven members of the EU.[31] As the accumulated obligations of EU membership grow, establishing tiers of members becomes more appealing: joining the Community in the 1990s "will require a far greater commitment to political and economic integra-

29. Nugent (1992).
30. For some of the preliminary discussion, "EU Enlargement: A Minority View," *The Economist*, February 26, 1994, p. 51; "Agenda for Euro-Reform," *Financial Times*, September 20, 1994, p. 19.
31. Nugent (1992, p. 321).

tion than joining the pre-1992 Community did."[32] The prospective accession of Poland, Hungary, Czechoslovakia, and other eastern European states—poorer, more agricultural, and threatening the voting weight of smaller existing members—makes a complex multispeed design even more likely.[33]

A multispeed Europe—or a Europe of "variable geometry"—has several meanings. Concessions to heterogeneity can take different forms that have different implications for a future EU. A multispeed Europe implies a common destination but different timing in reaching that destination, timing dependent on specified characteristics (such as level of economic development or per capita income.) This type of variable transitional arrangement is familiar from other international institutions. Differentiation among members is assumed to be temporary. A Europe à la carte, however, implies the possibility that there is not a common destination, that members may pick and choose those elements of the European policy regime that suit their preferences. The EU could become on this model an alliance of several "communities of the like-minded"—an economic and monetary union (already countenanced at Maastricht), a Social Europe (minus the United Kingdom), and so on. If one adds additional differentiation to accommodate the lengthy transition that some foresee for eastern Europe, the number of "communities" grows even larger.

Internal differentiation in an à la carte Europe or even a multispeed membership could impose several costs. Differentiation implies discrimination: the predictability and credibility of policy regimes desired by public and private actors could be eroded substantially, and the possibility for political conflict might increase. For those who see the future of the EU as federal and statelike, such differentiation must appear a step backward. Questioning of the EU's international role might also arise: negotiating partners may ask whether or on which issues the EU represents its members.[34]

These more profound issues of accommodating larger numbers of more heterogenous members will be addressed directly in the inter-

32. Sbragia (1992, p. 15).
33. On the issue of enlargement to the east and an architecture that might encompass it, see Baldwin (1994).
34. Lionel Barber, "Fresh Meat from Europe's Stable," *Financial Times,* September 8, 1994, p. 11.

governmental conference that will review the Maastricht Treaty in 1996. The debate opened explosively with the presentation of a report by the German Christian Democrats, who argued explicitly for a multispeed Europe and nominated the "hard core" of members that would be ready to press ahead with political, economic, and monetary union.[35] The multispeed Europe in the report seemed likely to persist for some time, becoming in fact a Europe à la carte. Despite strong negative reactions to the German report in those countries that were not nominated to the "high-speed" core, this crucial institutional dimension will necessarily be addressed by the EU in the 1990s. Politics and foreign policy press for enlargement; other economic and political realities make a unified policy regime for all of Europe less and less likely. In this respect, the EU has only confronted more explicitly the dilemmas of widening that appear in other regional arrangements.

DEEPER INTEGRATION AND RULE-BASED INSTITUTIONS. The two previous dilemmas of centralization and number are posed by divergent national preferences over domestic policy regimes and external objectives. The EU in 1992–93 also demonstrated the possibilities for contradiction between rule-based institutions and economic integration itself. The EMS was launched in 1979, at a time of "Euro-stagnation." Given the volatility in exchange rates since the breakdown of the Bretton Woods regime in 1971–73 and the unhappy experience of previous European attempts at economic and monetary coordination, few outside the European Community were optimistic about its prospects. The EMS core was a system of bilateral central rates between each pair of member currencies; members (apart from Italy) were obligated to intervene to defend those rates when they moved outside margins of 2.25 percent on either side of the central rate. This aspect of its operation represented a decentralized and rule-based system similar to that of Bretton Woods. In other respects, however, the EMS seemed to have surmounted the "constitutional revision" barrier that ultimately brought down the global monetary regime of fixed rates. Adjustment of the central rates in the EMS was subject to mutual agreement. At moments of policy divergence early in the history of the EMS—especially when the Mitterrand

35. Stephen Kinzer, "German Plan for Phased Union of Europe Provokes Controversy," *New York Times*, September 4, 1994, p. 11.

government in France embarked on policies of economic expansion that ran counter to the anti-inflationary stance of other members in 1981–83—central rates were adjusted in multilateral bargaining episodes that sought some measure of balance in adjustment burdens between surplus and deficit countries.[36] Rather than simply announcing unilateral measures, the convention was quickly established that changes in parities required the consent of the other members. Like Bretton Woods, the EMS not only constrained national policy through exchange rate rules; it also provided positive incentives in the form of facilities that provided financial support for members defending their parities during periods of adjustment.

This pattern of occasional realignment through multilateral bargaining began to disappear in the late 1980s. At the same time, as a result of the Single European Act, capital controls that had provided a hedge against pressures from the international financial markets were stripped away. The move toward economic and monetary union by means of gradual hardening of the exchange rate grid was portrayed by federalists as a necessary concomitant of the acceleration of economic integration after establishing a genuine common market. In fact, by most measures, the prospective EU was not an optimal currency area, and the principal motivations were political—promoting the federalist project and reducing the political resistance that economic integration might provoke in the presence of exchange rate volatility.[37] The gradualist model for proceeding to economic and monetary union was disrupted by successive exchange rate crises in 1992–93, crises that forced both a sharp widening of the bands of exchange rate fluctuation within the EMS and the departure of several key members from the exchange rate mechanism. EU governments and private market participants are still digesting the implications of this breakdown: whether it was driven by the lack of credible policy coordination in the aftermath of German reunification or an inherent fragility of systems grounded in pegged rates in the absence of capital controls. If the former, a credible policy coordi-

36. For early evaluations of the EMS, see Masera and Triffin (1984).
37. This political calculus is a principal motivation offered by Eichengreen (1994, pp. 108–09).

nation bargain might be reconstructed in the aftermath of the reunification shock. If the latter, Europe faces starker choices on the path to monetary union.[38] In either case, the advantages of a rule-based transitional system are called into question: the increment of credibility that external rules add seems diminished in the face of global financial markets that have grown markedly in scale and sophistication.

Regional Free-Trade Agreements and Institutional Variation

The EU is unusual on several institutional dimensions—scope of interdependent bargains and domestic linkages in particular. Its level of institutional elaboration is typically attributed to recognition of increasing spillovers related to heightened economic integration. The cyclical pattern of European institution building, the poor fit between European competences and principles of subsidiarity, and uncertainty over the degree of economic integration (for example, whether the EU is an optimal currency area) suggest that a powerful political dynamic has driven Europe's institutional history and overlain the demands of economic integration. The perception that policy spillover was powerful and spread from domain to domain, that coordination and institutionalization in one arena would eventually require similar measures in other policy spheres, was in itself politically powerful, however.

EFTA as an Institutional Alternative

EFTA, a contemporary of the European Common Market, embodied a different estimate of the degree of policy harmonization and institutional elaboration required by a free trade agreement.[39] The EFTA model prescribed "only the very lightest of institutional structures" and assumed that the market could handle economic integra-

---

38. This is the position taken by Eichengreen (1994, p. 111).

39. EFTA was founded when the Stockholm Convention entered into force on May 3, 1960. It may cease to exist when three of its remaining members enter the European Union in 1995.

tion almost single-handedly. It was a model that was "tough, reliable, and inexpensive in terms of loss of sovereignty."[40] The institutional formula of EFTA stands in contrast to the course chosen by the EU and remains a significant benchmark for the free-trade agreements (FTAs) of the 1980s and 1990s.

The international institutions of EFTA appear to be conventional: a council that served as the oversight body for the association and a very small secretariat and budget.[41] Nevertheless, EFTA's design proved to be flexible and capable of evolution in dealing with new issues as they arose. The Stockholm Convention establishing EFTA was definitely an incomplete contract that had been negotiated quickly; many points of disagreement were left for future negotiation and resolution. This was not a handicap, however. The council, a "diplomatic conference in permanent session," was able to deal with many of these outstanding issues over time, in a manner that did not disrupt the implementation of the FTA.[42]

EFTA did have two innovative institutional features by 1974. Its dispute settlement procedures were seldom used: only four formal complaints were submitted to the council under article 31. Curzon contended that members strongly preferred bilateral resolution of their dispute to arbitration by the council under a majority rule.[43] This finding reflects on the effectiveness of other dispute settlement mechanisms (DSMs) under GATT, particularly their ability to encourage dispute resolution without formal proceedings. EFTA also created a consultative committee, whose members, acting in their personal capacity, were drawn from those sectors most affected by the FTA. This device served as an important direct linkage to nongovernmental actors and a source of information for the association.

Despite its title, EFTA also moved, at a very early date, from dealing with at-the-border barriers to trade to nontariff barriers and behind-the-border distortions that influenced international exchange. Among the issues that it addressed were government subsidies to industry, public procurement, industrial standards, and restrictive

40. Price (1989, pp. 24, 26).
41. This account of EFTA's early history is drawn from Curzon (1974).
42. Curzon (1974, p. 42).
43. Curzon (1974, p. 52).

business practices. The strategies used by EFTA were decentralized ones (mutual recognition in the case of standards, for example). Members assumed broad obligations at best in these areas, implementation took place at the national level, and bilateral negotiations were used to resolve outstanding conflicts. As Curzon described, EFTA's pragmatic approach did not imply harmonization but was "simply an obligation to negotiate if a distortion arose and proved large enough to be irritating."[44] The principle of "frustration of benefits" limited claims of policy spillovers: domestic policy distortions were subject to negotiation if the expected benefits from free trade in manufactures were undermined.[45] EFTA also demonstrated a high level of trust among its member governments, a dimension on which later FTAs show wide variation. EFTA agreement to mutual recognition of product tests conducted at the facilities of other members depended on a level of comity that could not be attained in global organizations such as GATT.[46]

The new and revived FTAs of the 1990s display agendas that are more ambitious than simply removing barriers to exchange at the border, aiming in most cases at "GATT-plus" coverage if not a full-fledged common market. Although some nontariff barriers and sensitive sectors have been excluded from these agreements, governmental barriers at and behind the border have been targeted. The new generation of FTAs has also dealt with restrictions on capital movements and services, but they have left aside, for the most part, issues of labor mobility.[47] Despite their lengthening agendas, the institutional ambitions of these FTAs remain closer to those of EFTA than the elaborate structures of the EU. Within that reduced scope, however, both institutional innovation and variation require explanation.

Canada–United States Free Trade Agreement

The Canada–United States Free Trade Agreement (CUSTA) represented a bilateral effort to move beyond the then-stalemated

---

44. Curzon (1974, p. 223). On EFTA's approach to behind-the-border barriers, see Curzon (1974).

45. Curzon (1974, p. 145).

46. Curzon (1974, pp. 142–45).

47. A summary of the agenda items in these FTAs is given in de la Torre and Kelly (1992, pp. 13–17).

Uruguay Round agenda in GATT. In addition to the complete elimination of tariffs and the prohibition or restriction of nontariff barriers, CUSTA found it easier than GATT to liberalize services in a
bilateral setting. Investment, a historically sensitive issue between the
two countries, was also addressed in the agreement.[48]

The institutions of CUSTA overlaid an already dense network of
bilateral ties between Canada and the United States. One indicator of
the degree of acceptable intrusion into the politics of either side was
given in the FTA's provisions to exempt Canada from any U.S.
trade-restricting law unless Canada was mentioned explicitly in the
legislation. Even more remarkably, any legislation affecting Canada
had to be discussed bilaterally before passage.[49] The agreement itself
was dotted with a number of institutional means for consultation and
dispute settlement; it established a "cooperative regime" for dealing
with prospective trade conflicts.[50] Within this variegated regime for
"joint management" of the free-trade area, however, the innovative
DSMs contained in chapters 18 and 19 of the agreement have received the most attention.

Chapter 19 DSMs were, paradoxically, designed to deal with an
irreducible disagreement between the United States and Canada on
the issue of subsidies. One of the primary motivations for Canada to
enter the CUSTA negotiations was its desire to guarantee access to
the U.S. market and to restrain the use of American trade weapons.
For the United States, the more generous view of subsidies held in
Canada was in itself an unfair trade advantage. Dispute settlement
procedures were designed to provide a procedural means of reducing
conflict over the use of antidumping and countervailing duties while
negotiations on the knotty issue of subsidies continued. In certain
respects, such as the tight deadlines contained in chapter 19, the
DSMs were a precursor of reforms in GATT dispute settlement
under the Uruguay Round. In other respects, the new procedures
moved well beyond GATT and at the same time struck a compromise
between harmonization and mutual recognition.

Rather than attempting to harmonize approaches to dumping and
subsidies, dispute settlement under chapter 19 was carried out by

48. Lipsey and Smith (1989, pp. 319–321).
49. Lipsey and Smith (1989, p. 320).
50. Fried (1991, p. 382).

using each side's national trade laws as benchmarks. When an initial decision by an administrative agency was contested, review would not take place in the national courts but before a binational panel of five persons. That panel would assess only whether the administrative agencies had applied the relevant national law appropriately; it would not apply a new standard. Because the Canadians believed that American trade policy at the administrative level was influenced by political considerations and was not applied consistently, they saw gains from such binational review. The United States also gained review of certain Canadian trade policy outcomes that had not been subject to such review in the past.

An important step beyond even reformed GATT mechanisms was the enlarged access to the DSMs granted to private parties: any private party interested in the dispute could initiate a review. Hypothetically, it was possible that an importer damaged by the protection granted an import-competing industry could initiate a review against its own government under chapter 19 and then participate in the proceedings.[51]

The dispute settlement process was not accompanied by elaborate institutions: a small binational secretariat played a much less active role in the process than the GATT secretariat. Nevertheless, at least on the minimal criterion of resolving trade conflict, the mechanism seemed to have worked.[52] Three particularly contentious cases provoked efforts to overturn panel findings through an extraordinary challenge procedure contained in CUSTA. For those who had hoped for an additional level of appeal on the substance of particular panel decisions, however, the outcomes were a distinct disappointment. The extraordinary challenge committees (ECCs) have rejected the claims made against panel decisions and interpreted the ECC role narrowly—not as another stage of appeal on the merits of the case. In the most recent challenge of this kind, concerning softwood lumber, the ECC split two to one along national lines, with a Canadian majority upholding the chapter 19 panel. In response, the Coalition for Fair

51. Lowenfeld (1991, p. 271).
52. As of early 1993, forty-nine panels had been formed under chapter 19. Most panel determinations (sixteen versus six) have concerned U.S. agency decisions. Agency decisions have been affirmed nine times (five U.S. and four Canadian), and eleven panels have given split decisions; see Kelmar (1993, p. 183).

Lumber Imports in the United States has launched a constitutional challenge to the entire dispute settlement procedure under chapter 19, arguing that decisions regarding American law cannot constitutionally be applied by panels of private and (in part) foreign citizens. Paradoxically, innovation in dispute settlement—binational panels that assess the application of national laws and administrative procedures rather than international rules—has opened the chapter 19 procedures to this challenge.[53]

Dispute settlement under chapter 18 of CUSTA was a matter for the two governments represented on the Canada–United States Trade Commission; in that respect the rarely used procedures more closely resembled those of GATT. Even in this case, however, the procedures represented an advance over those of GATT (pre–Uruguay Round): time limits were strict; panel reports could not be blocked by either party; and panelists were chosen from a roster of individuals without government links.[54] The success of the intergovernmental dimensions of CUSTA can be measured by the absence of new trade conflicts between the parties outside the CUSTA procedures and the transfer of both chapter 18 and 19 procedures to NAFTA.

Harmonization of Policy Regimes and NAFTA

NAFTA, ratified in 1993, was more ambitious than GATT in its liberalizing agenda: its GATT-plus features were particularly notable for an FTA among one industrializing and two industrialized countries. A commitment to achieving free trade in agriculture between the United States and Mexico within fifteen years outstripped the modest achievements of GATT in this sector. The investment regime under NAFTA subjected most sectors to national treatment of NAFTA investors and ended most performance requirements. Other key service sectors—telecommunications, financial services, transport—were also liberalized, once again in contrast to the final balance sheet of the Uruguay Round.[55]

---

53. On the constitutional challenge, see Robert Keatley, "Canada Rivals Spur U.S. Timber Firms to Dispute Trade Law via Constitution," *Wall Street Journal*, September 23, 1994, p. A8; for arguments that the chapter 19 procedures are unconstitutional, see Kelmar (1993).

54. Fried (1991, p. 380).

55. For an evaluation of NAFTA's provisions, see Hufbauer and Schott (1993).

Despite these liberalizing benchmarks and despite differences in political regime that produced a lack of transparency between Mexico and its NAFTA partners, the NAFTA negotiations did not begin with high institutional ambitions. NAFTA's goals, like those in CUSTA, were largely a clearing away of obstacles to exchange, not the construction of a framework for positive policy coordination. NAFTA, in Hufbauer and Schott's phrase, was to be "integration of a lesser kind." Even the innovative institutions of CUSTA appeared at risk. Many were skeptical that Mexico, with its distinctive administrative and legal practices, could share the existing pattern of DSMs with Canada and the United States.[56] In fact, harmonization of Mexican practices—in part by voluntary action on the part of Mexico, in part through bargaining pressure from the United States—became a central issue in the negotiation and ratification of NAFTA. As a result, the scope of NAFTA expanded well beyond even a GATT-plus agenda and into policy realms that had typically been divorced from trade.

Despite these anxieties, NAFTA's DSMs closely resembled those of CUSTA in most respects and moved beyond them in others. Innovation is most marked in investor disputes: under NAFTA, investors can resort to binding international arbitration when a NAFTA government violates the investment provisions of the agreement. Rather than establishing its own DSM, disputes may be resolved under one of several international arbitral regimes. Panel decisions under the chosen regime are final. Enforcement would take place in the courts of NAFTA countries.[57]

Mexico's inclusion in the DSMs under chapters 19 and 20 of NAFTA (which closely resemble chapters 18 and 19 of CUSTA) marks a further step in the process of harmonizing its legal and administrative procedures with those of its neighbors to the north. Such alignment of Mexican practice with that of the United States had begun in some areas, such as intellectual property rights, even before NAFTA (and NAFTA will undoubtedly reinforce the ongoing trend).[58] Mexico's changes—culminating in a new intellectual property rights law in 1991—responded to bilateral pressures from the

56. See, for example, Lowenfeld (1991, p. 338).
57. DeBusk and Horlick (1993, pp. 22–26); Hufbauer and Schott (1993, pp. 80–81).
58. Zamora (1993, p. 415).

United States even before the NAFTA negotiations began. Just as the intellectual property rights sections of NAFTA will require further changes in Mexican treatment of intellectual property rights, the procedures concerning antidumping and countervailing duties under chapter 19 have forced a Mexican program to revise its trade policy procedures substantially, offering greater transparency and effective judicial review. At the same time, NAFTA offers a safeguard in its addition of a provision permitting consultations if a government is alleged to interfere in the panel process.[59]

Mexico in these instances chose harmonization of its domestic legal and regulatory system to gain the benefits of participation in DSMs crafted along the lines of CUSTA. More significant and certainly more politically sensitive was broadening of the NAFTA negotiations beyond trade issues, conventionally defined, to include environmental and labor policies. Given strong domestic preferences to maintain national practices in these areas (and to thwart further demands for harmonization by the United States in other spheres), Canada and Mexico preferred the narrower definition of trade negotiations, limiting the inclusion of issues that did not directly impinge on trade. The Bush administration shared this view of an appropriate agenda, but the president's need for fast-track negotiating authority in 1991 offered organized labor, environmental lobbies, and their allies in Congress an opening for expansion of the NAFTA agenda. The Bush administration moved some distance in "greening" NAFTA: it included explicit provisions in the agreement that members could enact environmental standards stricter than international ones and that existing health, safety, and environmental standards would be maintained (that is, no regulatory "race to the bottom" would be permitted). The Bush administration also designed an integrated environmental plan for the Mexican–U.S. border area to deal with transborder environmental spillovers. Finally, the Bush administration advanced a modest degree of institutionalization in the form of a North American Environmental Commission.[60]

The election of Bill Clinton as president of the United States placed labor and environmental objections to NAFTA on the preratification

---

59. Hufbauer and Schott (1993, p. 103); DeBusk and Horlick (1993, p. 34).

60. Hufbauer and Schott (1993, pp. 92–99); on environmental issues in NAFTA, see Wilkinson (1994).

agenda. Clinton had made his support of NAFTA conditional on the negotiation of side agreements to deal with each of these issues. The agreements that were finally announced included a panoply of institutions with far fewer delegated powers than environmental and labor activists had hoped. Although it is too soon to offer even a preliminary estimate of institutions that are in certain cases still in formation, the outlines of the environmental and labor regimes under NAFTA are clear.

Inserting environmental and labor standards into the NAFTA negotiations elicited the pattern of national preferences described in chapter 1. Given distributional conflict in the United States, the U.S. government preferred harmonization to American practice; Mexico and Canada resisted this threat to their national autonomy. The compromise in the side agreements resembled the logic of the CUSTA-NAFTA DSM. Because labor and environmental standards in the three NAFTA states were not dissimilar on paper, the side agreements centered on enforcement of those standards. Any member of NAFTA could initiate consultations if it believed that another member government was not enforcing its *national* environmental or labor law. If such consultations did not reach a mutually satisfactory resolution, then further procedures that resemble those under chapters 19 and 20 could be instituted, including an arbitral panel, the assessment of fines (to be devoted to environmental improvement), and ultimately the suspension of benefits under NAFTA. The authority of the Commission for Labor Cooperation is less than that of its environmental counterpart; the independent power of the environmental secretariat is greater as well, because it can undertake independent investigations. In both cases, however, nongovernmental parties and private individuals do not have the opportunity to initiate DSMs to enforce national environmental or labor laws. Nongovernmental organizations can make submissions to the secretariat, which can in turn request a response from a member state. To further circumscribe private access in enforcement of environmental or labor law, the side agreement explicitly stipulates that the parties to NAFTA cannot provide a right to take action in their courts against other members for failure to enforce environmental laws.[61] To date,

61. North American Agreement on Environmental Cooperation, part vi, article 38. Article 37 forbids "undertaking environmental law enforcement activities in the territory of another Party."

American labor unions have made more use of the side agreements than American environmentalists, supplementing their organizing activities alongside Mexican counterparts with complaints lodged under the labor side agreement to NAFTA.[62]

Incorporation of these relatively elaborate institutions in NAFTA raises the issue of inevitable policy spillover and a widening of the scope of NAFTA over time. The drive to harmonize labor and environmental standards in North America was neither inevitable nor dictated by economic prescription, however: the linkage was political, and it was driven by perceived losses from economic integration. Whether a similar political process could force a further expansion of scope in NAFTA is not yet clear. One candidate for inclusion—exchange rate coordination—is unlikely on purely economic criteria, because both factor mobility and mutual trade dependence remain relatively low in North America, and supply shocks are not highly correlated across North America.[63] Two political dynamics could force a move toward collective exchange rate management, however. From the industrialized country (particularly the United States) side, demands for exchange rate stability could arise if a sharp Mexican devaluation produced an import surge and demands for protection in the United States. Exchange rate volatility could, under those circumstances, endanger the regional trade agreement. Alternatively, the Mexican government could press for an enhancement in its own credibility through attachment of the peso to the dollar in a clear-cut and visible way.[64] Either dynamic might override skepticism based on economic givens, just as it did in the move toward economic and monetary union in Europe. A limited degree of support for the Mexican peso was put in place with U.S. cooperation at three times during 1993–94. A line of credit was provided to the Mexican authorities to deal with pressures on the exchange rate from possible political shocks (a failure of the United States to ratify NAFTA, the assassination of presidential candidate Colosio, and unforeseen Mexican election results). These episodes of support, however, were not linked formally to NAFTA and, in two cases, included central banks of western Europe

62. Allen R. Myerson, "Big Labor's Strategic Raid in Mexico," *New York Times,* September 12, 1994, p. D1.
63. Bayoumi and Eichengreen (1994).
64. On this dynamic, Maxfield (1993).

and Japan.[65] The financial crisis that followed Mexico's abrupt devaluation of the peso in late 1994 raised the exchange rate and financial corollaries of NAFTA in even sharper form. The Clinton administration's proposal of financial guarantees to Mexico could imply institutional innovations in the longer run beyond those in the original agreement.

The pressure toward greater harmonization—driven primarily by political demands—as opposed to a less institutionalized and decentralized future for the FTA is only one dimension on which NAFTA faces an institutional dilemma. The issue of widening to a regional grouping of larger numbers also holds institutional implications. The Summit of the Americas (December 1994) endorsed the construction of a Free Trade Area of the Americas (FTAA) and agreed that negotiations should conclude by 2005. The FTAA would include investment liberalization as well as the removal of barriers to trade; its agenda also moves beyond that of the Uruguay Round to deal with competition policy. The precise modalities for achieving the FTAA remain unclear, however. The announcement at Miami that negotiations would begin for Chilean accession to NAFTA suggested that joining NAFTA would remain one route to free trade for at least some Latin American countries. The Clinton administration also made clear that provisions of NAFTA would remain the benchmark for an eventual FTAA in such controversial areas as environmental and labor standards. Existing subregional groups (such as the Common Market of South America, MERCOSUR) could also become building blocks in a wider arrangement, or regional groups could converge on common standards before coalescing into an FTAA.[66] Which of these avenues toward the FTAA will be dominant is unclear, and the institutional implications—whether DSMs only or more elaborate institutional arrangements—are also unresolved.

Pacific Asia: The Arc of Institutional Development

The Pacific region—whether defined to include the United States and Canada or limited to East Asia—represents a profound anomaly for any argument that posits a strong relationship between economic

65. Anthony DePalma, "Mexico's Trading Allies Play Financial Bodyguard," *New York Times*, September 12, 1994, p. D2.

66. Steven Greenhouse, "U.S. Plans Expanded Trade Zone," *New York Times*, February 4, 1994, pp. C1, C10.

interdependence and institutional strength. The intraregional trade bias within East Asia is strong when compared with that of other regions such as the Western Hemisphere or the EU; when a Pacific or APEC region is constructed (including the United States and Canada), the intraregional bias appears to be the strongest among potential regional blocs.[67] Although East Asian trade interdependence declined after 1945 from its very high levels during the era of imperialism before World War II, the late 1980s saw a burst of cross-investment within the region related to revaluation of the Japanese yen (and the currencies of the East Asian newly industrializing countries).[68] Nevertheless, the institutional framework for this regional economic dynamic, however *region* is defined, is slender and declines on every dimension as the definition of region expanded from bilateral or subregional ties to the Pacific as a whole.

On nearly every dimension of institutional development—strength, scope, centralization, domestic political linkages—Pacific institutions lie at one end of the international distribution. Historically, the Pacific has been characterized by bilateral institutions structured by "hub-and-spoke" relations with the United States. The Association of Southeast Asian Nations (ASEAN), a long-standing subregional grouping, has enjoyed considerable success as a diplomatic community and lobby within the larger international order but much less success as a locus for economic collaboration. Repeated proposals for a Pacific-wide organization have resulted in APEC, an institution that possesses only a small secretariat and is governed by no strong rules, procedural or substantive, and, more recently, the ASEAN Regional Forum to deal with security issues. Even the Australia–New Zealand Closer Economic Relations Trade Agreement (ANZCERTA), the most successful free-trade arrangement in the region and one with an ambitious deeper integration agenda, is almost defiantly lacking in formal institutional development.

The Asia-Pacific region provides plausible evidence, not for a single institutional design based on cultural ("Asian way") determinants or a peculiar strategic environment, but for one of the hypotheses advanced in chapter 1. Decentralized and informal institutional innovation may result from two different informational environments:

67. Frankel (1993).
68. Petri (1993).

on the one hand, scarce and expensive information that requires substantial information gathering before additional institution building can occur, and, at the other end of the arc of information, plentiful and cheap information about the preferences and reputations of partners, in which decentralized, reputation-based systems may be sufficient.[69] The two ends of this arc are both represented in the international institutions of the Pacific region.

ANZCERTA: Economic Integration with Political Transparency

ANZCERTA provides strong support for Harry Johnson's contention that ambitious programs of trade liberalization do not require an elaborate institutional infrastructure. One of ANZCERTA's architects has proclaimed it, with only a little exaggeration, "perhaps the world's most advanced and developed bilateral trade agreement," with some features that move beyond even the 1992 program of the European Community.[70] An initial phase of shallow integration began after 1983, when the governments on either side of the Tasman Sea embarked on programs of extensive economic liberalization, including trade liberalization. ANZCERTA, in its first phase, was both part of and an external support for those programs of liberalization.

After the 1988 review, the agreement entered a second and much more ambitious phase in dealing with behind-the-border barriers to exchange and issues of deeper integration. The agenda of shallow integration was accelerated, resulting in the removal of nearly all barriers to a single binational market by July 1990. Antidumping procedures for goods were abolished in favor of reliance on competition law, a shift that has been urged for the *next* round of global trade negotiations. The Protocol on Trade in Services achieved fast-track status by using a negative list approach (services were included in liberalization unless explicitly excluded) and applying the standard of national treatment in market access. Harmonization took place in business law and regulatory practices, customs procedures, government purchasing, and technical barriers to trade. Subsidies, so contentious an issue between the United States and Canada, occupied a very low profile in negotiations between Australia and New Zealand,

---

69. Petri (1993).

70. See comments by Grame Thomson in "Australia–New Zealand Trade Agreement," *The Globe* (Summer 1991), p. 4.

probably because both governments were committed to unilaterally and radically reducing subsidies. After the 1992 review of ANZCERTA, other issues were proposed for the agenda. New Zealand wanted to include investment, but the Treaty of Nara with Japan committed Australia to extending any investment benefits negotiated under ANZCERTA to Japan. Business on either side wishes to see greater harmonization of taxation, but tax authorities have been reluctant to part with their prerogatives up to this point. Finally, the issue of exchange rate coordination has been broached, but Australia has been reluctant to overload the bilateral agenda with issues that touch more directly on national sovereignty.[71]

The institutional frame for this comprehensive approach is a continuous review process that has extended the agenda of ANZCERTA, imposed requirements for transparency in national policymaking on issues that might affect the other party, and included provisions for immediate consultation if requested by either government (the Services Protocol). The governments avoided a reliance on binational institutions for monitoring and enforcement of the agreements; considerable effort was made to create a self-enforcing agreement or, more precisely, an agreement that could be enforced by private agents that were directly affected by any infringements.[72] Despite (or perhaps because of) the absence of intergovernmental machinery of a permanent sort, ANZCERTA has not been plagued by disputes.

The particular form of this agreement, one that deals directly with complex behind-the-border issues, can be explained in at least three ways. First, relative lack of concern over possible defection by one trading partner and the absence of institutional means to deter such defection could be a function of the relatively low mutual trade dependence between New Zealand and Australia. ANZCERTA (trans-Tasman) trade forms a lower share of the regional partners' external commerce than in any other industrialized FTA (including EFTA, EC, and CUSTA).[73] Defection in this view would be of relatively little significance to the overall economic prospects of either New Zealand or Australia. A second explanation, for Australia's institutional stance

---

71. The provisions of ANZCERTA are discussed in Department of Foreign Affairs and Trade, Australia (1988); Thomson and Langman (1991); Cobban (1992).

72. Thomson and Langman (1991, p. 204).

73. See the chart in de la Torre and Kelly (1992, p. 18).

at least, is a belief on the part of the larger trading partner that New Zealand will converge on Australian practice through market pressures. (Such calculations did not prevent the United States from attempting to accelerate harmonization in Mexico under NAFTA and the side agreements, however.)

Finally, a more extensive institutional structure is viewed as unnecessary when relations between the economic partners are characterized by a high degree of political transparency and shared perceptions that underlying preferences were aligned. Just as the European Community could entertain mutual recognition with its risks of institutional competition and a regulatory "race to the bottom" in the context of a high degree of comity, so could Australia and New Zealand forswear institutionalization of their trade agreement. Both left-of-center reformist governments had staked their political futures on the success of their liberalization programs, which they had pursued over domestic political resistance. Neither government was the target of strong immediate pressures to deviate from that policy path, at least in its external dimension. The trans-Tasman game was one of almost pure assurance: only transparency was required. In another sense, however, this explanation is too imprecise: in other situations, perceived alignment of preferences, a democratic political order guaranteeing transparency of the policy process, and a high level of information did not erase the need for at least modest institutional innovation. It is not clear from this single case whether the arc tracing institutional development is based on an abundance of information, transparency of decisionmaking (linked to political institutions), or simple alignment of preferences. Additional instances in which these competing explanations can be teased apart are required to determine which of these effects is dominant and how they may reinforce one another.

Institution Building in the Pacific: The Outlines of APEC

Although the Pacific region is hardly an institutional desert, no regionwide institutions (East Asian or Pacific) have achieved prominence since 1945, and those subregional institutions that have enjoyed success have all shared certain common characteristics: they have displayed little delegation to formal organizations and few clear injunctions; they have been narrow in scope; and they have been built from the bottom up over time rather than through episodes of constitution making. ASEAN, perhaps the most successful of these institutions, has enjoyed its greatest prominence as a diplomatic community dealing with such issues as the Vietnamese invasion of Cambodia. Its success in negotiating a free or preferential trading area over the decades of its existence has been disappointing. Its most recent initiative, the ASEAN Free Trade Area (AFTA) agreed at ASEAN's 1992 summit, will take effect over fifteen years; it does not include agricultural or services trade. It also does little to address the important issue of nontariff barriers.[74] Familiar delays in the governmental negotiations for AFTA have, however, met with pressure from regional business elites to move forward more rapidly, perhaps the first time that private support for liberalization has been exhibited in this way.[75] ASEAN has avoided the construction of an extensive permanent or formal institutional core, apart from a small secretariat. Other subregional arrangements display the same institutional biases. Minitrading areas (MTAs), such as the growth triangle among Singapore, Malaysia, and Indonesia, have not developed common institutions. Most of the MTAs planned for the region will have only a loose intergovernmental structure, with a prominent role awarded to the private sector in planning infrastructure and joint investment.[76]

A Pacific-wide economic institution was finally established with the formation of APEC in 1989. Several changes made a Pacific regional organization, however ill-defined, more acceptable by the late 1980s. The United States, hostile in the past to initiatives that might undermine its central place in the cold war bilateral arrangements of the region, had accepted that a multilateral economic initiative could support its position and also provide a minor counter to the newly energetic European Community. The principal barrier to Pacific institution building in the past had been resistance from the developing countries of the region, particularly ASEAN.[77] They remained suspicious of any impressive institutional design, but their

74. Michael Vatikiotis, "AFTA, Mark II," *Far Eastern Economic Review*, October 21, 1993, p. 74.

75. John McBeth and Rigoberto Tiglao, "ASEAN Profitable Partnership," *Far Eastern Economic Review*, July 28, 1994, p. 30; Rodney Tasker, Adam Schwarz, and Michael Vatikiotis, "ASEAN Growing Pains," *Far Eastern Economic Review*, July 28, 1994, pp. 22–23.

76. McBeth and Tiglao, "ASEAN Profitable Partnership," p. 30.

77. Testimony on this point is given by Rostow (1986, p. 106).

own turn toward external liberalization in the 1980s and their concern over access to the American market eased acceptance of a low-key arrangement. In its first years, APEC has served several modest roles in the region: a center for research and information sharing and a focus for joint positions on global trade negotiations.

The APEC Summit in November 1993 signaled U.S. interest in moving the organization forward in its institutional development and its common economic agenda. The Eminent Persons Group (EPG) produced an ambitious report in preparation for the summit, one that urged setting a timetable and target date for deciding to achieve free trade in the Pacific region and also included an extensive set of trade and investment facilitation recommendations dealing with behind-the-border obstacles to exchange. The recommended measures included an investment code, competition policy, product standards, environmental policies, and rules of origin. At the same time, the EPG report emphasized the need to align APEC measures with the global trade regime and downplayed the need for rapid institution building. It argued for an "effective dispute settlement mechanism" (without describing what concrete obligations such a DSM would address) and for putting in place a small, permanent secretariat and an "effective decisionmaking" process. The report itself and later comments by its chair suggested continued skepticism among many members on the need for a Pacific-wide set of institutions. The institutional recommendations of the EPG—an increase in status for the secretariat, a shift in ministerial responsibility to economics and trade ministers, collective financing of the secretariat—were very modest.[78]

The 1993 summit itself demonstrated for some that APEC "has become a negotiating forum rather than a purely consultative body."[79] The principal accomplishment of the meeting of foreign and trade ministers of APEC was to formulate a common negotiating position for the final stages of the Uruguay Round. In other respects, there was little evidence of support for the ambitious EPG agenda at Seattle. The assembled political leaders accepted annual summits and authorized implementation of EPG recommendations that overlapped with APEC work-in-progress; finance ministers also began to meet

78. APEC (1993, p. 22).
79. Bergsten (1994).

regularly to discuss macroeconomic issues (the first meeting was held in March 1994). Little enthusiasm was expressed for enhancing the institutional capabilities of APEC.

The second APEC summit (November 1994) endorsed a region-wide program for liberalizing trade and investment. Accepting recommendations of the second EPG report (August 1994), the heads of government not only agreed to a long-term goal of "free and open trade and investment" in the Asia-Pacific region, they also approved a nonbinding set of principles to govern investment among members. The multispeed timetable set for liberalization stretched far into the future: industrialized countries committed to complete liberalization by 2010 and developing countries by 2020. Although investment was included in the summit commitments, ambiguity remained on several points—the inclusion of agriculture and services in the liberalization agenda and the designation of developing countries. Nevertheless, a political commitment at the highest level had been achieved for a "GATT-plus" agenda of liberalization that included both removal of barriers to trade at the border and behind-the-border measures such as harmonization of standards and a review of competition policies. The consensus among APEC members was surprising in light of past hesitation at accepting formal commitments of this kind.

Despite APEC's apparent progress on the road from consultative forum to free trade arrangement, its institutional evolution is likely to be slow. The summit seemed to signal a shift toward the American and Australian view of APEC's future: clearer obligations to undertake specific policy changes within an active negotiating forum. Asian members appeared to resist this vision and favored a more informal institution built from the bottom up in an evolutionary fashion.[80] This contrast was apparent in the most important institutional innovation proposed in the second EPG report: a dispute mediation service. This far more modest analog to the DSMs of NAFTA and GATT was predicated on the absence of either "agreed rules" or "comparability of laws" within APEC.[81]

Linked to different views of APEC's institutional future were different strategies for ensuring APEC consistency with the global trade

---

80. On these divergent viewpoints, see Charles Smith, "Bump Ahead," *Far Eastern Economic Review*, September 15, 1994, p. 77.

81. APEC (1994, p. 23).

regime. The EPG advanced several routes for ensuring "open region-alism." The American position appeared to rely on further negotia-tion at the global level, coupled with extension of the benefits of any APEC liberalization on a reciprocal basis to nonmembers. As a fur-ther safeguard, open accession to the "like-minded" (those willing to accept the obligations of membership) served to ensure that the dis-criminatory effects of reducing intra-APEC barriers would be mini-mized. Some Asian participants favored a stronger version of open regionalism—extending the benefits of APEC liberalization on an unconditional most favored nation (MFN) basis to those who were not members. The second EPG report accepted that members could extend benefits unilaterally on an unconditional basis if they chose to do so.[82]

The first EPG report offered three explanations for the weakness of regional institutions in the Pacific: reliance on private actors to drive the process of regional interdependence forward (but that feature has characterized most regional arrangements outside the Soviet bloc); heterogeneity along a North-South divide as well as different models of political economy (which hardly distinguishes it from NAFTA); and finally, the reliance of the region on reasonably effective global institutions. Delicacy prevented mention of another explanation based on the arc of information (or transparency): APEC members have in the recent past been actively hostile to one another, and in some cases, relations are still marked by mistrust. Aversion to institutional-ization within ASEAN (and other minilateral arrangements in the region) could be attributed to developing country concerns over sovereignty and national policy autonomy. Equally important, how-ever, is a lack of transparency in regimes that, in some cases, remain authoritarian and could recall a history of political and military conflict.

The movement toward a broad-scope FTA within ASEAN and APEC's commitment to a liberalization timetable may mark movement along the arc of information toward more highly institutionalized inter-action. APEC may remain in the initial phase of information gathering and testing of preferences, however. Until its members are convinced of a closer alignment of preferences, particularly in the absence of great power leadership that is difficult for either Japan or the United States,

82. APEC (1994, p. 30).

further institution building in APEC will be slow at best. The current institutional structure relies on working groups, a process of consultation, a small secretariat, and annual summits. Whether this institutional design is adequate for the ambitious liberalization agenda that APEC has set and whether these institutions can move APEC's members along the arc of information and transparency are open to question. If the arc is indeed one of information, then a process of working groups and information sharing similar to that of the Organization for Economic Cooperation and Development may prove effective; if the arc is one of realigned preferences and political transparency, the region may have to move toward less heterogeneity for successful APEC institutions to take hold.

Chapter 4

Conclusion

A RICH variety of institutional forms has emerged to accompany closer economic integration. The degree of variation belies a simple economic model that predicts necessary convergence on a particular institutional design or consistent movement along any institutional dimension. The evolution of these institutions seems to confirm that recognition of economic spillovers and perceptions of joint gains from coordinated or harmonized policies are shaped by political and cognitive dynamics, as are the particular institutional choices that have been made.

Change in Institutional Dimensions

Economic integration has been accompanied by a more centralized design, greater enforcement powers, clearer rules, and wider scope in some international institutions, but those features have not appeared consistently over time or uniformly across institutional settings. Deeper economic integration does seem to spur innovation in constructing linkages to the domestic politics of members. Nearly all of the institutions considered have also been forced to deal with the dilemmas of larger membership, which often represent a tension between wider and deeper economic integration.

Strength

Few institutions show a consistent pattern of "strengthening," whether defined by a more formal structure with an organizational

117

core or an enlarged role awarded to third-party enforcement. At the global level, the General Agreement on Tariffs and Trade (GATT) that emerged from the Uruguay Round was clearly strengthened through negotiation of a World Trade Organization (WTO) and improvements made in its dispute settlement mechanisms. The connection between those changes and the agenda of behind-the-border issues that were part of the Uruguay Round agenda is less than clear, however: the *widening* of GATT and a desire by its powerful members to avoid free riding by developing countries that had become significant traders may have played a more important role. The history of the international monetary regime demonstrates even more forcefully that economic integration—in this case, financial integration—need not be accompanied by stronger institutions.

Transformation of the European Community into the European Union (EU) in the Maastricht Treaty seems to represent a clear strengthening of several European institutions. But the near-collapse of the European monetary system in 1992–93 and the lukewarm or hostile reaction to the Maastricht project in successive political tests has brought a questioning of the apparently inexorable European progress toward a more centralized and statelike set of institutions. The EU remains unique among regional arrangements in the degree of delegation to its permanent institutions. That delegation is not fixed and could be circumscribed, but it has inserted those institutions into intergovernmental bargaining in a continuous and active way. Much of the apparent "strength" of the EC does not lie in the formal attributes of its institutions or in their enforcement capabilities, however, but in the web of interdependent bargains over which they preside and their less apparent and dense connections to the domestic politics of the member states. No other regional institutions exhibit these characteristics to the same degree. Perhaps the greatest anomaly for any attempt to associate economic integration and strength of institutions lies in the Pacific, where economic dynamism and growing regional integration have produced only weak institutions such as Asia-Pacific Economic Cooperation (APEC).

Although any broad trend toward strengthening international institutions on the above criteria cannot be discerned, behind-the-border issues have produced one widespread institutional innovation that does imply a strengthening of institutions: the development or extension of monitoring mechanisms. In nearly every institutional case examined, strengthening took the form of enhanced monitoring capabilities.[1] The trade policy review mechanism of GATT, article IV consultations in the International Monetary Fund (IMF), and a host of notification and review mechanisms in regional arrangements are all indicative of a role for institutions that moves beyond serving as a simple information exchange. Increased emphasis on monitoring and surveillance of national policies is not, however, necessarily coupled with enhanced and centralized enforcement capabilities. Even in those cases in which strengthening is apparent—such as GATT—enforcement, if it should take place, will remain decentralized and in the hands of member states.

This trend toward "strengthening" of this sort can be explained in part by the particular characteristics of collaboration in the era of deeper integration. Because more and more states prefer liberalized international outcomes (given their increasing dependence on international markets of all kinds), their preferences produce strategic interactions that are more like games of assurance or coordination than collaboration games—the risks of opportunistic defection from the central liberalizing bargain are reduced. Nevertheless, in bargaining over behind-the-border issues governments often undertake to change administrative and regulatory practices that are opaque to outsiders and may not be fully under the control of those forging the agreement. This is particularly the case when private practices (such as anticompetitive business practices) are at stake. Government capabilities may be inadequate for fulfilling the agreed bargain. The "deeper" the demands for change and the less visible, the greater the need for outside monitoring of the bargains that are reached. Transparency must extend well beyond tariffs and other familiar policies that may impede exchange at the border. International monitoring in effect imposes reputational costs on governments if they fail to invest in adequate capabilities of their own to fulfill their international bargains.

Substantive versus Procedural Rules

Often related to institutional strength, particularly in legalist views of international institutions, is the development of substantive rules. Rule-based systems have often been seen as possessing important

---

1. This feature also figures prominently in the environmental institutions considered in Haas, Keohane, and Levy (1993, pp. 402–03).

advantages of credibility because they are "simple but rigid." Institutions based on substantive rules have proved to be fragile entities, however. Systems based on substantive rules "are unlikely to cover all contingencies, and, as soon as conditions change, countries are unlikely to stick to the rules."[2] The history of the IMF and the collapse of the par value system is a prominent case in point. The difficulty in adapting a rule-based system in the face of unexpected change or shocks resembles the dilemmas of devising means for amending constitutions in emergencies.[3]

The brittle character of substantive rules in the face of international economic change has meant that such rule-based institutional design remains relatively rare in dealing with behind-the-border issues. Devising substantive rules to cover these issues is made even more difficult because, on the frontier of deeper integration, normative consensus and cognitive convergence simply do not exist. The gains from harmonization are disputed; the causal connections between particular national practices and impediments to access are also subjects of conflict. Institutions such as the Japanese *keiretsu*, which are perceived in the United States as sources of unfair competitive advantage and in Japan as legitimate institutional innovations, exemplify such deeper disagreements.

In such cases, attempting to force conflict into existing regimes or even to apply existing principles or rules from such institutions may be premature and counterproductive. Instead, procedural rules can be devised to trigger dispute settlement mechanisms (DSMs) or negotiations in which substantive consensus does not exist. Purely procedural means can be used to determine the facts and to alleviate political pressures and, through continuing scrutiny and negotiation, determine which common norms or rules, if any, can be borrowed or developed to cover the issues in conflict. The DSMs of the European Free Trade Association (EFTA) embodied an obligation to negotiate, even without an accord on common rules, when a member complained about a nontariff distortion. The GATT DSM could serve the same purpose under the rubric of "nonviolation nullification and impairment." The Organization for Economic Cooperation and Development (OECD) has also served as a useful negotiating forum to forge a principled consensus among the industrialized countries on

2. Dominguez (1993, p. 363).
3. On this point, see Elster (1994, p. 24).

issues such as agriculture and investment. The Canada–United States Free Trade Agreement's DSM served this function in part: it was intended as a stopgap measure while negotiations on the politically contentious issue of subsidies continued between the two countries.

Centralized and Decentralized Institutional Models

The balance between centralized coordination or harmonization of policy and more decentralized models such as mutual recognition is at the core of debates over international responses to closer economic integration. Those choices are, in fact, at the midpoint of a spectrum of choices between reservations of national autonomy and unification or federation (complete unification of policy regimes). Even as economic integration increases, national governments have been careful to reserve islands of autonomy that are of particular political sensitivity: this has been the clear pattern in most free-trade agreements completed in the past decade.

The international institutional and domestic political prerequisites of more and less decentralized models of collaboration allowing more or less variation in national policy regimes are not as clear cut as they may appear. Harmonization has well-known drawbacks and fairly stiff prerequisites for success. In conditions of bargaining among relative equals in capabilities, the perceived joint payoff in terms of enhanced efficiency and increased market scope should be high, and the pre-existing differences among national norms and rules should not be too wide. Also, success is more likely if the net investment of domestic interests in particular practices or rules is low or negative (the beneficiaries from international harmonization are more influential than the losers). Common knowledge and shared causal models also contribute to successful harmonization by establishing clear causal connections between harmonization and particular economic outcomes as well as demonstrating the threat from alternative policies (for example, protection) if harmonization does not succeed. Many harmonization attempts in the cases described were interest driven, however: domestic politics in the more powerful negotiating partner set the agenda. The prerequisites listed above were not apparent; in particular, the causal links between freer international exchange and particular domestic policies were not shared by the participants.

The institutional requirements for harmonization are high in the negotiating phase; the informational requirements are also likely to be high. After harmonization is negotiated, the international institutions associated with it are dependent on the underlying structure of the harmonization bargain. In some cases, harmonization outcomes resemble a coordination game, and subsequent institutions are limited to information sharing. As already described, however, the types of harmonization attempted (or demanded) under conditions of deeper integration often impinge on sensitive national policies. Monitoring and surveillance capabilities are necessary and have often been expanded; DSMs have also been elaborated.

Mutual recognition—a device adopted by the European Community to accelerate the clearing of remaining impediments to a common market—has been widely misinterpreted. The turn toward mutual recognition was in part a response to the perceived failure of explicit harmonization under the decision rules of unanimity then used by the European Community. Acceptance of the degree of decentralization implied by mutual recognition depended on an existing context of substantial harmonization or convergence of national policies. As a strategy for managing conflict over the degree of acceptable national policy divergence in conditions of closer economic integration, the prerequisites for mutual recognition—domestic and international—may be as demanding as those of harmonization. Within the EU, national preferences are seen as broadly aligned on key policies; a high degree of decisionmaking transparency and similarity in domestic politics (including common democratic regimes) reinforces the willingness to concede a greater measure of national policy autonomy. A second feature predisposing Europe toward more decentralized institutional forms is a perception that any regulatory "race to the bottom" or process of policy competition will be slow or may not occur at all, given national preferences for similar public goods. Finally, distributional conflict over the process of integration and the threat of institutional competition is eased in Europe by access to the political process on the part of all key economic actors (particularly labor).

The European shift toward the more decentralized institutional model embodied in mutual recognition and renewed debate on the principles of subsidiarity provide support for the arc of information hypothesis. Decentralized institutional evolution and design is most likely when levels of information among governments and societies are low (and an initial confidence-building role is awarded to institutions) and again when information about the preferences of other governments is plentiful. Europe's highly centralized institutions may seem less necessary as economic integration and political understanding produce an increasingly information-rich environment. Even in these contexts, national policies may still require a degree of surveillance by negotiating partners, to ensure that "diversity" does not become "disguised protection" or that competition and competitive pressures do not become unacceptable "social dumping" or "environmental dumping." This function is performed by both the European Court of Justice and the Commission in the EU, with considerable assistance from national institutions.

At the global level and in other regional arrangements, the reserved spheres of national policy autonomy are larger. Nevertheless, one can perceive a muted version of the decentralized institutional model taking shape in different forms. As Sykes suggested in his consideration of standards negotiations under GATT, "policed decentralization" seems to be the model that is emerging: wide bands of harmonization agreed upon internationally, within which national authorities can forge covenants of mutual recognition or pursue their own policy objectives subject to a set of broadly applicable legal constraints.[4] Those principles—such as the "least-restrictive means" test—have come to characterize the principles used by the European Community and national courts as well. In the North American Free Trade Agreement (NAFTA), a hybrid form characterizes the labor and environmental side agreements: explicit harmonization of national standards was not politically feasible, but surveillance of national implementation of national legislation is included. EFTA, in an earlier era, was able to rely on decentralized institutional design because of high levels of transparency and trust; for the same reasons, the Australia–New Zealand Closer Economic Relations Trade Agreement (ANZCERTA) in the Pacific is the clearest contemporary example of dealing with behind-the-border policies through highly decentralized means. In the case of Australia and New Zealand, the degree of preference alignment and national transparency is so great that little institutionalization has been required.

4. Sykes (1995, pp. 118–130).

Scope

As economic integration advances, the functional scope of inter-national institutions might be expected to expand through the political economy of issue spillover—the linkage of outcomes and policy coordination in one area to those in another. For the institutions examined in this study, such spillovers and the resulting expansion of functional scope are shaped by political dynamics and cognitive assumptions more than the inexorable demands of economic integration. The relationship between trade liberalization and exchange rate coordination, for example, has been on the European agenda since the late 1960s. One of its primary motors in the early years of the European Community was the Common Agricultural Policy and the threat that exchange rate instability posed to that intricate political bargain. At the global level, the linkage also became prominent through a political stimulus: the rise in protectionism in the United States in the early 1980s during a time of exchange rate overvaluation. The threat of protectionism in the face of macroeconomic misman-agement stimulated both the launch of the Uruguay Round and the reinvigoration of macroeconomic policy coordination from the Plaza accord onward. Equally significant—and discussed in greater detail below—the costs of cross-issue spillover are seldom clear, and the gains from additional coordination or harmonization in new functional areas are seldom specified. Many of the costs can also be offset by private actors using private mechanisms, such as forward exchange markets, without additional government policy coordination.

Expansion of scope may require a cognitive shift on the part of participants to accept linkages that were previously invisible or suppressed. The long march of services into the GATT system, as described earlier, matches this cognitive or epistemic underpinning for widening of scope: investment and intellectual property were seen as "trade-related" only after such change.

Finally, an international political dynamic has been important in widening the scope of institutions in many of the cases discussed. More powerful actors, with capabilities across several issue-areas, may press for a widening of scope to exploit their ability to link issues and gain more favorable outcomes. Actors with fewer capabilities across issue-areas, however, may prefer functionally specific institutions and resist efforts to widen the scope of institutions. Conflicts of this kind emerged between the United States (and the other industrialized countries) on the one hand and the developing countries on the other at the start of the Uruguay Round. Canada and Mexico resisted the widened scope of NAFTA for similar reasons: they saw the lever of American market access being used to harmonize policies in sectors that they wished to reserve for national policy.

In those cases in which widened scope appears desirable or is demanded politically, the widening can be accomplished by absorbing some of the new issue-areas into an existing organization (the GATT model) or by establishing closer links between existing organizations that share responsibility for the issue-areas in question. The mixed success of IMF–World Bank coordination and the untested promise of collaboration between the Bretton Woods institutions and the new WTO raise doubts about the second strategy, given entrenched issue-specific operating procedures and protective attitudes toward policy turf on the part of established institutions. The conflict between environmentalists and GATT highlights the need to deal with questions of scope early on, ideally before the negotiation of new environmental agreements. As new issues are added to the international economic agenda, more careful design to deal with issues of scope—through expansion of existing institutions or establishing new links among those institutions—will be required.

Finally, scope poses the issue of institutional competition. Overlapping functions among international institutions are usually taken as a costly and unnecessary lack of tidiness. A certain measure of competition among international institutions produces a more open structure, however, and may well produce more innovative solutions as new issues enter the international agenda. The availability of GATT was central to the liberalization in the telecommunications sector; the United States used the regional card to move along a new agenda in the Uruguay Round. Although the search for new roles may signify a simple desire for institutional survival, that search may also produce a better fit between issue and institution.

Number

The dilemmas presented by large and growing membership numbers are confronted by both global and regional institutions. These dilemmas also play an important role in the choice between global and regional (or plurilateral) institutions. For political reasons (such as enhancing political stability through intensified economic exchange or concern over free riding on the benefits of bargains that are effectively public goods), large-number institutions have become more attractive. The widening of membership, however, typically decreases the efficiency of decisionmaking, because it necessarily increases the diversity of national systems and the heterogeneity of interests represented. Deciding which issues to deal with in the Uruguay Round and which in plurilateral or bilateral negotiations among groups of the like-minded illustrates one face of this dilemma; at the regional level, debate over widening the EU and extending NAFTA displays another face of the same issues.

Two strategies can be used to deal with the dilemmas of number. One is the design of institutional devices to enhance the efficiency of collective action. The IMF, through a system of weighted voting and special majorities (to protect the interests of key members or blocs of members), has been able to move far more expeditiously (when the most powerful members agree) than other global organizations. Institutional reforms in GATT should also speed decisionmaking if the members use the new institutions. The easing of the consensus rule in dispute settlement, the effective delegation of a greater role to panels of experts, and the setting of clear time limits in the process should expedite a previously cumbersome process. Establishing a clear organizational core to which collective responsibilities can be delegated should provide an additional increment of effectiveness. The architecture of a wider EU will undoubtedly include different decisionmaking rules to ensure that enlargement does not mean institutional stalemate.

Such institutional devices have limits: if larger numbers of members mean a sharp increase in heterogeneity, adjustment in decision rules may not suffice. A second strategy—decomposition—may be required. It has appeared in two forms. Within large-number institutions, multispeed arrangements are becoming more common. In the Uruguay Round agreements of GATT/WTO, different transition periods have often been set for industrialized and developing countries. Enlargement of the EU to the east will almost certainly include a long period before full membership. The EU already displays "variable geometry," to the distress of some members. The United Kingdom has opted out of the Social Charter, and the economic and monetary union can move forward without the participation of all members.

The second means of decomposition—plurilateral or regional arrangements—poses different risks. In part because of the unevenness of economic integration, groups of like-minded and more closely integrated economies have often banded together to strike bargains and construct institutions to monitor those bargains. The principal constraint on the discriminatory effects of those bargains remains GATT article XXIV, widely criticized as an inadequate and often-ignored hurdle for regional arrangements to surmount. Apart from tougher notification and surveillance of small-number bargains of all kinds (not simply regional arrangements), the emerging governance structure requires clearer rules of consistency between global institutions and their obligations on the one hand and small-number bargains that will be struck in increasing numbers on the other. Strengthening GATT article XXIV would be one desirable step. The debate within APEC over open regionalism suggests other means of reducing the negative effects of small-number collaboration on outsiders. One is open accession: willingness to admit any country that satisfied certain criteria for membership. Another is a guarantee that any benefits will be extended to nonmembers through reciprocal bargaining or on an unconditional most favored nation basis. As the preceding discussion of scope suggests, consistency should be "horizontal" across issue areas as well as "vertical" (between global and regional or minilateral bargains). The best strategy for formulating rules of consistency is through umbrella agreements at the global level that continue to permit small-number experimentation without producing costly fragmentation.

Domestic Political Linkages

Post-1945 international institutions began as clearly intergovernmental entities: in most cases, governments served as watchful gatekeepers between international and domestic politics. Increasingly, however, national governments are designing means for using domestic groups to strengthen international institutions and maintain cooperative bargains. Domestic groups are demanding additional access to international decisionmaking as stakeholders if not shareholders. And the institutions themselves discover new forms of influence, most evident in the EU, through the elaboration of direct links to national societies.

Given an increased demand for monitoring capabilities, private economic agents (businesses encountering barriers to entry, for example) can provide very useful "fire alarms" given the complexities of mounting "police patrols" to oversee implementation of agreed changes.[5] Few international institutions, apart from the European Community, award direct access to nonstate actors, although the arbitration provisions of NAFTA suggest a greater willingness to contemplate this possibility. Domestic trade law often provides such access but without international oversight to curb abuses. Given the interests of both governments and many organized groups in increasing access of this kind, connections between international institutions and nongovernmental actors are likely to increase. A second avenue for enhancing monitoring is to devolve responsibilities on domestic allies within member states. Without such allies, monitoring national commitments may be nearly impossible. The tacit alliance forged between lower national courts and the European Court of Justice is one striking example of this strategy. Involving implementing agencies in the original international bargain may enhance monitoring as well.

Dynamics of Institutional Variation: Knowledge-Driven and Interest-Driven Accounts

Knowledge-driven change has played an influential role in the institutional choices made under deeper integration. It is commonplace to remark on the dramatic shift toward opening to the international economy and market-oriented policies that has characterized domestic political choices in the past decade. Many of those policy choices were directed toward the familiar removal of barriers to international exchange. The implications for other domestic institutions and practices were often sidestepped or ignored. As other domestic policies are called into question, however, or the effects of international competition become evident, market-oriented norms that dominate global economic institutions and new regional free-trade agreements are challenged by at least three different cognitive or

5. McCubbins and Schwartz (1984).

ideological orientations based in national politics. One is simple nationalism—a defense of national autonomy as a good in itself. This discourse was apparent in the final days of the Uruguay Round negotiations as the French government mobilized opposition to American "domination" of cultural industries worldwide. It has also provided a source of opposition to free trade with the United States in Canada. A second strand of opposition is the familiar coalition of those who may lose economically from intensified economic integration. A core participant is labor in the industrialized countries, but their program is no longer simple protectionism. Instead, in an era of widely accepted openness, international harmonization "upward" to current national standards becomes a new demand: institutional competition is opposed as "unfair trade." Finally, a third strand of opposition that is likely to grow in influence during the 1990s derives from "new regulators": those who seek to protect health, consumer safety, and above all, the environment. These forms of regulation are widely viewed as legitimate, and some, although not all, of their proponents are deeply skeptical of international liberalizing trends.

Given this array of potential opponents, one is impressed at the weakness of the base of knowledge that has been developed in support of the program of continued economic integration and institutional development to further that integration. In particular, and in contrast to international environmental institutions, the level of knowledge creation on these issues within international economic institutions has not been impressive. The research agendas of many of the dominant institutions remain those of shallow integration (particularly the Bretton Woods institutions), in part because their clients are increasingly the developing and transitional economies.

On two points, a better base of knowledge would at least sharpen the debate between the opponents and proponents of further economic integration, even if it did not resolve all extant political differences. Knowledge on these issues would also assist in more informed choices about appropriate international institutions. One is the not-so-simple question of the gains from more coordinated or explicitly harmonized policies. Too often, harmonization is suggested as necessary for unspecified economic gains or to remove distortions or transactions costs whose levels are rarely estimated. Much of what is known about the costs of technical barriers to trade is "impressionistic and anecdotal."[6] On a much larger issue, European integration, Lawrence noted the wide range of estimates given for the benefits of the 1992 move to a single market.[7] Ehrenberg's review of labor policies in the highly integrated American market suggested that explicit harmonization of many important labor market policies does not seem required to obtain extensive benefits from market integration.[8] In an area that has received extensive attention from researchers, optimal currency areas, Krugman recently declared that estimates of the microeconomic benefits of a common currency were "a matter of metaphor and slogans rather than worked-out models."[9]

Another area of intense conflict in which additional knowledge would offer substantial benefits is the causal connection between economic integration and the behavior of private economic agents. The limited research that has been done so far suggests that fears of footloose firms seeking "pollution havens" are overdrawn and that financial services firms will not relocate en masse to the Cayman Islands. Nevertheless, many of the political anxieties surrounding integration (and the efforts to deal with supposed effects through harmonization) are based on only vaguest notions of how firms and workers will respond to the new conditions.

Finally, international institutions could play an important role—as the OECD already has—in transferring "best national practice" for dealing with the issues of international integration across national borders. By enhancing a process of national learning, such knowledge transfer would also obviate the need for extensive efforts at explicit harmonization and increase levels of international transparency. The Basel Committee of central bankers and regulators is a good example of how this process can work in a highly informal institutional setting.

Interest-driven politics has been central to this account of international institutions under new conditions. Rather than reviewing in detail the ways in which the play of domestic interests has affected each of the international institutions considered, two principal and often overlooked routes should be stressed. Much of the agenda

6. Sykes (1995, p. 10).
7. Lawrence (forthcoming).
8. Ehrenberg (1994).
9. Krugman (1993, p. 20).

arising from economic integration—demands for national policy harmonization, claims of "unfair" trade, fears of system friction—has been driven by domestic politics. The knowledge base for many of the claims—that particular domestic practices constitute barriers to exchange, for example—has been slender. As hypothesized in chapter 1, however, those threatened by economic integration have moved demands for harmonization to their own national standards to the top of the political agenda. Old-style demands for simple closure or national policy autonomy no longer receive much hearing when such a wide spectrum of opinion is convinced of the reality of "globalization." Harmonization also receives support from two other sources: some of those engaged internationally and benefiting from international integration may also prefer harmonization (although differing on what should be harmonized and at what level). Even more significantly, groups within the target country may also have an interest in external pressure to move their own domestic agendas forward. Increasingly, the distributional conflicts that produce national demands for both policy change abroad and international institutional changes to oversee it are becoming part of a transnational pattern of alliances and bargaining. Those transnational political links, on environmental and labor issues, for example, may change both the domestic and international politics surrounding economic integration.

The interest-driven model of institutional choice also suggests that domestic cleavages resulting from economic integration may contribute to the monitoring and implementation of international bargains. As described above, those national policies that are at issue—such as regulatory policies—are often difficult for international institutions to monitor. The availability of domestic political allies becomes invaluable in extending the reach of international oversight and sustaining international commitments.

Evaluating International Institutions

Three conventional views of international institutions were described in chapter 1. The naive institutionalism of many political scientists holds that "more is more" in institutionalization: interstate cooperation is most likely in a more highly institutionalized environment. The legalist perspective presses for a view of future international institutions that is relatively homogeneous: clearer rules, stronger powers of enforcement, formal rather than informal. This judicial or quasi-judicial model of institutions sometimes puts forward a criterion of success that is not connected to conflict resolution but is based instead on whether the "cases" made it to "court." This image of international institutions neglects not only the wide array of conflict resolution devices illuminated by comparative law but also the politics, international and domestic, that underlie international institutional design.[10] As Judith Shklar remarked in her brilliant polemic on legalism, there is a distaste in the legalist view for the "politics of negotiation, expediency, and arbitrariness . . . the adjudicative process is held up as the model for government, the substitute for politics."[11] Finally, economists often bring to the investigation of international institutions an implicit standard of judgment—maximizing global economic welfare through increasing the gains from trade—and an explicit strategy of reducing or removing political impediments to exchange.

These three conventional views converge, for somewhat different reasons, on a common institutional model: strong, formal, centralized, rule-based institutions are most likely to confirm cooperative bargains among states that are necessary for reducing barriers to trade and investment. International institutions are weak-form states, and they will become more successful as they become more statelike.

In contrast to these views and this model of institutional evolution, the institutional array described in this study suggests several very different criteria for evaluating international institutions. One is flexibility and adaptability: international economic institutions confront major shocks and constant change in their environment. Whether they will be robust in the face of that change is an important question, given the costs of creating new institutions. The criterion of adaptability or robustness points toward an institutional model that is more likely to be decentralized and avoids the rigidities of substantive rules.

Taking direct cognizance of a changing environment suggests a second criterion: a field of international institutions that displays a diversity of institutional designs. Rather than a single model of institutional evolution, broadly similar to the federalist image of the

10. See Shapiro (1981).
11. Shklar (1964, p. 18).

European Community, diversity and competition among institutions should be seen as a significant means of ensuring that the most efficient institutions are selected. Under rapidly changing economic conditions and domestic political demands, those institutions that remain close to the requirements of their members are more likely to succeed and survive.

Finally, national diversity is often slighted in the normative judgments of those who endorse further economic integration. Institutions are given high marks for realizing the (often unspecified) joint gains from the freer movement of goods, capital, and labor, for removing impediments to exchange and lowering transaction costs. This "harmonization bias," however, leaves out any positive estimate of national diversity itself. As Herring and Litan remarked in their treatment of financial regulation, the "net benefit of variety and uniformity" in national systems requires assessment.[12] Once again, a more open and evolutionary view of the future would assign considerable value to national experimentation and institutional innovation. Harmonization risks eliminating national differences that may have beneficial global effects. Squaring national diversity with the fewest possible impediments to exchange is precisely the line of international debate at the present moment. In their design international institutions represent those competing values. The tension between them is likely to persist in a world of deepening economic integration and continued political fragmentation.

12. Herring and Litan (1995, p. 82).

Comments

Robert O. Keohane

Miles Kahler has written an admirable book, which contains both insightful and extensive descriptions of major international economic institutions, such as those associated with the General Agreement on Tariffs and Trade (GATT), the International Monetary Fund (IMF), the European Union, and the North American Free Trade Agreement (NAFTA), and fascinating brief discussions of an array of lesser-known institutions, from the European Free Trade Association (EFTA) to the Canada–United States Free Trade Agreement (CUSTA), Asia-Pacific Economic Cooperation (APEC), and the Australia–New Zealand trade agreement (ANZCERTA). Kahler's work develops a clear theme: that economic integration has not led to a single, functionally driven pattern of institutional change. Economic integration does not necessarily lead to centralized, rule-based institutions that expand their scope. On the contrary, we observe a great deal of institutional variety, which was not predicted by legalistic, economistic, or naively institutionalist interpretations of international institutional change.

The evidence for this argument about institutional variety is overwhelming. Even the European Union (EU), the contemporary international institution with both the greatest legal authority and the deepest links to domestic politics, has disappointed those of its supporters who expected continuous movement toward a federal state.

Robert O. Keohane is Stanfield Professor of International Peace, Center for International Affairs, Harvard University.

The EU's progress has been quite impressive, but "institution building in Europe has followed a jagged trajectory," despite growing
economic interdependence and strong political incentives for closer
cooperation. The IMF has had a more checkered career: indeed, the
principal features of the early IMF regime "crumbled in part because
of increased international financial integration." On the other hand,
predictions of GATT's death by such pundits as Lester Thurow were
at best premature, as, like the legendary phoenix, it was reborn in
1994, with more elaborate rules and a larger organizational embodi-
ment. And regional institutions such as CUSTA and NAFTA have
taken on what might have seemed ten years ago to be improbable
forms, with procedures that arguably impinge on the legal sovereignty
of the United States.

However, it is more difficult to provide a coherent interpretation of
a complex reality than to demonstrate the inadequacy of simplistic
predictions. Yet it is also more challenging. Kahler has ventured
beyond his specific descriptions and his debunking of apolitical arguments about institutional development to put forward one descriptive
hypothesis about overall patterns and three causal hypotheses. He
also identifies three important sources of tension, which he does not
develop into hypotheses. In this brief commentary I highlight Kahler's
hypotheses, which are put forward in various places in his book, and
subject them to scrutiny from three perspectives: the clarity of the
concepts on which they rest, particularly the notion of institutional
"strength"; the value conflicts that institutional change reveals; and
the evidence supporting Kahler's causal inferences. Finally, I focus on
three tensions that Kahler identifies and suggest that they may point
to fruitful directions for future work.

Kahler's Hypotheses

Kahler's central descriptive hypothesis is that "the pattern that best
captures [the observed variety of international institutions] is policed
or monitored decentralization." Such monitored decentralization involves "wide bands of harmonization agreed upon internationally,"
within which mutual recognition and national discretion can coexist
in a variety of ways. Not only does this pattern fit the facts, it also
makes theoretical sense, given the combination of continuing state

authority and potential gains from coordination that confronts the world political economy. Fragmentation of authority proscribes serious third-party enforcement, apart from exceptional situations; gains from coordination mean that governments need information about others' preferences, politics, and capabilities. International institutions reduce the costs of making agreements and provide information that both eases coordination and increases the credibility of others' commitments in situations of collaboration. As Kahler notes, we find similar patterns of monitoring by international institutions in other issue-areas: environment, human rights, and arms control provide three examples. Kahler puts forward three causal hypotheses:

1. The Advantages of Flexibility: "Institutions based on substantive rules have proved to be fragile entities." Rapid economic change and shocks overtake them. In contrast, flexibility and openness, as in GATT, may increase the usefulness of an international institution. This hypothesis is based principally on the contrast drawn in chapter 2 between GATT, portrayed as successful, and the IMF, depicted as unable to adapt effectively to changes in financial markets.

2. The Value of Domestic Linkages: "A strategy of establishing significant domestic linkages—political allies that will persist over time—often offers a higher probability of success [than a strategy of monitoring rules] in influencing national policies." In chapter 4, this hypothesis is modified so as to view domestic linkages and monitoring more as complementary rather than as alternative strategies: "A second avenue for enhancing monitoring is to devolve responsibilities on domestic allies within member states."

3. The Arc of Information Hypothesis: Decentralized institutions are most likely to be formed both when information is scarce and hard to get and when it is plentiful and cheap; centralized institutions are more likely to exist when moderate levels and cost of information are the rule.

Policy Implications and the Paradox of "Success"

These three hypotheses point toward the policy implications of Kahler's argument. He implicitly advises leaders to build flexible institutions, properly adapted to informational conditions, that emphasize procedures rather than substantive rules and that rely on supportive domestic constituencies. GATT provides the ideal example in support of this argument. The IMF is a negative example—too rule-oriented for its own good. Although the success of the rule-oriented and fairly centralized EU might seem to be a counter-example to hypotheses (1) and (3), Kahler claims that "the European shift toward the more decentralized institutional model embodied in mutual recognition and renewed debate on the principles of subsidiarity provide support for the arc of information hypothesis."

These policy implications depend on Kahler's definition of success or of strength and are only as good as the causal inferences that underlie them and the values being pursued by international institutions. Even if success and strength are equated, their definition is ambiguous, as discussed in the following paragraphs. But they should not be equated—as the following section on values argues. Quite apart from these conceptual difficulties, the causal inferences on which Kahler's policy implications rely should be regarded more as speculative hypotheses than as firm conclusions based on substantial evidence.

Success seems to be defined in terms of both persistence—robust institutions are more successful than brittle ones—and what Kahler denotes as "strength." Conceptually Kahler is clear on what strength means: "the effect that institutions have on the behavior of states." But measuring strength is difficult, and Kahler is ambiguous on whether the role of formal institutions in monitoring and enforcement is a reasonable proxy for strength. At different points such an equation seems to be accepted (chapter 2 on GATT), denied (chapter 2 on the IMF), or treated ambiguously (chapters 1 and 4).

The ambiguity in the conceptualization of strength, or success, seems to reflect a more profound paradox in the hypothesis of the advantages of flexibility. GATT is said to exemplify this hypothesis—it successfully capitalized on its flexibility—but the indicator of its very success is precisely the tighter rules and stronger formal institutions authorized by the outcome of the Uruguay Round. But it is hard to have it both ways: to point to the success of a decentralized GATT as evidence of the value of decentralization, but to define success as a transformation of GATT into a more centralized, formal institution! If "it is not clear that a more centralized, formal, and rule-based institution would have proved so robust and adaptable to changing world economic circumstances," why should we view GATT's formalization as a sign of success? Kahler's ambivalence is evident in his formulation of the paradox. Since I think that his point is insightful, I raise the issue less to point out a contradiction in the argument than to help illuminate an ongoing ambivalence in our notion of strength or success where international institutions are concerned.

Policy Implications and Value Conflicts

It is important to remind ourselves, as Kahler does, that with respect to international institutions more is not necessarily better. Polemics about the role of IMF structural adjustment policies on income and wealth inequality, and of the World Bank on the natural environment, have made it clear that international institutions can be associated with harmful effects—to people and to their environment. Hence, in value terms, strength and success must be differentiated from one another: an institution can be strong without being successful in a normative sense.

One issue that Kahler discusses illustrates quite well the subtle impact of value conflicts, the roles that international institutions may play, and thus the need for differentiating between strength and success. This is the question of trade and the natural environment, which became salient in United States debates over NAFTA and GATT. These debates, as Kahler indicates, involved two communities with few links between them: the international trade network and the community of environmentalists. Each has a nightmare.

The trade community has feared that environmentalists would join with protectionist industries to enact discriminatory legislation with a phony green hue. Such coalitions would be like the apocryphal alliances between Baptists and bootleggers under prohibition: both groups supported prohibition, but for entirely different reasons.

For their part, environmentalists, who lost the first round when the new GATT was approved by the U.S. Congress, worry that in decisions over domestic environmental regulations a stronger GATT would privilege free trade over environmental protection at the margin. Environmental regulations will now have to meet criteria of "necessity" and "proportionality," which are inherently quite subjective, and the panels making these judgments will be constituted principally by trade lawyers, not by environmentalists. Furthermore, a stronger GATT will clearly restrict the ability of the United States to impose sanctions unilaterally on other countries for allegedly failing to adopt adequate environmental policies.

Both of these nightmares have some basis in reality. Rent-seeking industries will indeed search for any protective coloration they can find. Hence the fear of free traders was justified. But so is at least one version of the environmentalist nightmare—and given the overwhelming forces favoring liberal trade, it is more likely to come about.

As Kahler indicates, the problem is not that there is likely to be a "race to the bottom" on environmental protection. It is also not a matter of the United States being outvoted by other less environmentally sensitive countries (as is sometimes suggested by environmentalists). Nor will the most legalistic nightmares of the environmentalists come to pass: international law exists in the shadow of domestic political power, and trade panels (like the Tuna-Dolphin Panel) that seek to enact their preferences without respect for political realities are likely to find their actions negated—as even the much stronger United States Supreme Court found (for example, after the Dred Scott decision before the Civil War or during the New Deal).

The real difficulty for environmentalists is different. The new GATT rules incorporated in the World Trade Organization will constrain the potential coalitions that environmentalists can construct, thus limiting their ability to win domestic political battles. The prospect of authorized trade sanctions will deter Congress from adopting environmental legislation that can be interpreted as discriminatory, thus preventing the formation of even relatively mild "Baptist-bootlegger" coalitions, such as are evident in U.S. fleet-based fuel economy standards for automobiles. At the margin, some political battles will therefore be lost by environmentalists when they cannot triumph without gaining the support of certain industries that would benefit by adding discriminatory provisions to legislation.

In other words, the legalistic ideal of nondiscriminatory environmental legislation will sometimes be politically infeasible. Requiring nondiscrimination may therefore preclude certain types of environmental regulation: a real trade-off exists. For people who are in the abstract both free traders and environmentalists, whether one favors a strengthened GATT therefore depends on the weighing of these values. But it won't do to ignore the trade-off: political battles are fought at the margins, and at the margin, the new GATT will surely strengthen forces favoring liberal trade at the expense of domestic regulators, including environmentalists. Judgments on the "success" of international institutions, and policy advice about how they should be encouraged to evolve, depend as much upon one's values as upon professional judgments about causality or institutional design.

Policy Implications and Causal Inferences

As noted, Kahler's policy implications are only as good as the causal arguments behind them. Although I share many of Kahler's views, I wish to caution that evidence for his causal inferences is slight. As noted, the major evidence for the Advantages of Flexibility hypothesis lies in the contrast between GATT and the IMF. But GATT rules apply to trade, whereas the IMF sought in its heyday to peg exchange rates. Financial markets are much more volatile than markets for goods, as the exchange rate crises of the 1970s, the collapse of the exchange rates of the European Monetary System during the early 1990s, and the run on the Mexican peso late in 1994 indicate. Social democratic governments in Europe have had more trouble with financial markets than with making liberal trade consistent with government regulation.[1] If we had an example of a flexible, informal institution that had successfully coordinated exchange rates, and of an inflexible, formal-legalistic institution that had failed to regulate trade, the evidence for the Advantages of Flexibility hypothesis would be stronger. As it is, the hypothesis should only be seen as just that: a speculation induced by the experiences of GATT and the IMF, but one as yet untested.

The Domestic Linkages hypothesis surely reflects a real correlation: international institutions with powerful domestic allies certainly have more impact on state policies than do those without such constituencies. However, this correlation does not imply that institutional *strategy* is the source of this variation. Even if the leaders of all international institutions pursued optimal strategies, some institutions would have stronger domestic linkages than others, owing to

1. See Garrett (forthcoming). The problem here is one of omitted variable bias: a variable different from flexibility/formality, but correlated with it (that is, whether the institution deals with trade or finance), could be causing the observed variation in outcomes. See King, Keohane, and Verba (1994, pp. 168–82).

differing configurations of underlying interests. If differing interests were responsible for different outcomes, then the hypothesis attributing variation in success to different strategies would be false.

The Arc of Information hypothesis, intriguing as it is, also suffers from lack of evidence. Post hoc, it seems to make sense, and to be consistent with our understanding of how international institutions function: when levels of information are very low, formal and centralized institutions cannot be constructed; when they are high, such institutions are unnecessary. But no a priori theory tells us what levels are "high" or "low." Indeed, the hypothesis is purely inductive: we observe decentralized institutional arrangements both at the low end of the arc of information (for example, APEC) and at the high end (for example, EFTA and ANZCERTA). The EU is very centralized on a comparative basis, yet there is a high level of information within it; so even on an ex post basis the correlation posited by the hypothesis is not perfect. Furthermore, even the correlation that is observed could, as Kahler acknowledges, be accounted for on the basis of interests rather than information. Levels of information among states are to some extent endogenous to interests: that is, the closer are state preferences, the more willing the states are likely to be to share information with one another, since they will be less inclined to use information to exploit one another. More evidence will be required to distinguish the impact of information from that of interests, and owing to endogeneity, it will not be easy to sort out the effects of each.

Tensions: Themes to Pursue

Finally, Kahler identifies three areas of tension with respect to international economic institutions that in my judgment could provide openings for further research:

1. Plurilateralism versus Free Riding. Kahler perceptively points out a tension created by the entry of many more states as significant players in the world economy. The expansion in the number of players produces pressure for plurilateralism: efficiency of decisionmaking would be enhanced with fewer bargainers at the negotiating table. However, free riding—benefiting from others' acceptance of obligations without assuming obligations oneself—becomes a more serious problem as economic activity becomes less concentrated. Hence, "the

tension between these two dynamics has probably intensified" as economic integration has increased. In his conclusion, Kahler offers some valuable suggestions for institutional devices to deal with these dilemmas.

2. The Centralization-Decentralization Dynamic. Kahler is somewhat ambiguous as to whether "centralization" refers to standards that apply uniformly to a single area (as in EC attempts at harmonization in the 1970s and early 1980s; see chapters 3 and 4) or to third-party enforcement (see chapter 1). His most interesting argument uses the uniformity definition and posits a cycle of decentralization and recentralization: "Greater decentralization may in the long run produce another cycle of policy transfer to European institutions." International institutions typically seek to regulate areas with both diverse national political institutions and preferences, on the one hand, and significant externalities or potential gains from exchange, on the other. It would not be surprising under these circumstances if awareness of externalities and gains from exchange led to centralization, against which adversely affected interests and institutions would react. But such a reaction could lead again to damage from externalities and losses from failure to coordinate, precipitating new efforts at centralization. Surely Kahler is right in believing that much of the history of the EU could be interpreted in light of this centralization-decentralization dynamic; it would be interesting to see how far it could be extended.

3. Diversity and Interinstitutional Conflict. At the end of his book, Kahler endorses institutional diversity: "diversity and competition among institutions should be seen as a significant means of ensuring that the most efficient institutions are selected." That is, there should be a market for institutions; let the most efficient win! However sympathetic one may be to the sentiment, it is not so easy to secure efficiency. Competition can lead to bitter battles for organizational turf, such as those that have been endemic to the United Nations system and that are now causing serious difficulties in implementing coherent environmental policies. Like individuals, states do not seek efficiency, but only to secure their interests; however, there is no "invisible hand" provided by a competitive, price-driven market to ensure efficiency in world politics. (Even in economics, after all, a perfect market is an ideal type—albeit one that is approximated more frequently than in politics.) It would be worthwhile to explore system-

atically the costs and benefits of interinstitutional competition and diversity in contemporary world politics.

Conclusion

Kahler has provided us with a magisterial survey of how economic integration and international institutions impinge on one another. There is surely much more to be done; but his emphasis on politics, contingency, and institutional choice suggests a more fruitful direction than adhering to naive institutionalism, whether based on idealism, legalism, or a simplistic economic functionalism. For students of international institutions in the world political economy, the variety of forms of institutions, the complexity of linkages between international institutions and societies, and the strategic relations among institutions all provide the basis for challenging work in the years ahead.

References

Asia-Pacific Economic Cooperation. 1993. *A Vision for APEC: Towards an Asia Pacific Economic Community.*

———. 1994. *Achieving the APEC Vision: Free and Open Trade in the Asia Pacific.*

Alesina, Alberto. 1993. "Comment." In *A Retrospective on the Bretton Woods System,* edited by Michael D. Bordo and Barry Eichengreen, 397–401. University of Chicago Press.

Alter, Karen J., and Sophie Meunier-Aitsahalia. 1994. "Judicial Politics in the European Community: European Integration and the Pathbreaking *Cassis de Dijon* Decision." *Comparative Political Studies* 26 (January): 535–61.

Anderson, Kym, and Richard Blackhurst. 1992. *The Greening of World Trade Issues.* University of Michigan Press.

Baker, Richard W., and Gary R. Hawke, eds. 1992. *ANZUS Economics: Economic Trends and Relations among Australia, New Zealand and the United States.* Westport, Conn.: Praeger.

Baldwin, Richard E. 1994. *Towards an Integrated Europe.* London: Center for Economic Policy Research.

Barton, John H. 1984. "Two Ideas of International Organization." *Michigan Law Review* 82 (April-May): 1520–32.

Bayoumi, Tamim, and Barry Eichengreen. 1994. "Monetary and Exchange Rate Arrangements for NAFTA." *Journal of Development Economics* 43 (February): 125–65.

Bergsten, C. Fred. 1994. "Sunrise in Seattle." *International Economic Insights* 5 (January-February): 18–20.

Birdsall, Nancy, and David Wheeler. 1993. "Trade Policy and Industrial Pollution in Latin America: Where Are the Pollution Havens?" *Journal of Environment and Development* 2 (Winter): 137–49.

Black, Stanley W. 1991. *A Levite among the Priests: Edward M. Bernstein and the Origins of the Bretton Woods System.* Boulder, Colo.: Westview.

Bordo, Michael D. 1993. "The Bretton Woods International Monetary System: A Historical Overview." In *A Retrospective on the Bretton Woods System,* edited by Michael D. Bordo and Barry Eichengreen, 3–98. University of Chicago Press.

Bretton Woods Commission. 1994. *Bretton Woods: Looking to the Future*. Washington, D.C.

Bryant, Ralph C. Forthcoming. *International Coordination of National Stabilization Policies*. Brookings.

Burley, Anne-Marie, and Walter Mattli. 1993. "Europe before the Court: A Political Theory of Legal Integration." *International Organization* 47 (Winter): 41–76.

Castel, J. G. 1989. "The Uruguay Round and the Improvements to the GATT Dispute Settlement Rules and Procedures." *International and Comparative Law Quarterly* 38 (October): 835–48.

Center for Economic Policy Research. 1993. *Making Sense of Subsidiarity: How Much Centralization for Europe?* London.

Charnovitz, Steve. 1993. "Environmentalism Confronts GATT Rules." *Journal of World Trade* 27 (April): 37–54.

Chayes, Abram, and Antonia Handler Chayes. 1993. "On Compliance." *International Organization* 47 (Spring): 175–206.

Cobban, Murray. 1992. "The Australia–New Zealand Economic Relationship: The Role of CER." In *ANZUS Economics*, edited by Richard W. Baker and Gary R. Hawke, 149–66. Westport, Conn.: Praeger.

Cooper, Richard N. 1989. "International Cooperation in Public Health as a Prologue to Macroeconomic Cooperation." In *Can Nations Agree?*, edited by Richard N. Cooper and others, 178–254. Brookings.

Corbett, Richard. 1992. "The Intergovernmental Conference on Political Union." *Journal of Common Market Studies* 30 (September): 271–98.

Corbo, Vittorio. 1991. *Report on Adjustment Lending II*. Washington: World Bank.

Cowhey, Peter F. 1990. "The International Telecommunications Regime: The Political Roots of Regimes for High Technology." *International Organization* 44 (Spring): 169–200.

Cowhey, Peter F., and Jonathan D. Aronson. 1993. *Managing the World Economy: The Consequences of Corporate Alliances*. New York: Council on Foreign Relations Press.

Crockett, Andrew. 1989. "The Role of International Institutions in Surveillance and Policy Coordination." In *Macroeconomic Policies in an Interdependent World*, edited by Ralph C. Bryant and others, 343–80. Washington, D.C.: International Monetary Fund.

Curzon, Victoria. 1974. *The Essentials of Economic Integration: Lessons of the EFTA Experience*. St. Martin's Press.

Dam, Kenneth W. 1982. *The Rules of the Game: Reform and Evolution in the International Monetary System*. University of Chicago Press.

Davis, Gerald F., and others. 1990. "Contracts, Treaties, and Joint Ventures." In *Organizations and Nation-States*, edited by Robert L. Kahn and Mayer N. Zald, 25–29. San Francisco: Jossey-Bass.

DeBusk, F. Amanda, and Gary N. Horlick. 1993. "Dispute Resolution under NAFTA: Building on the U.S.–Canada FTA, GATT and ICSID." *Journal of World Trade* 27 (February): 21–42.

Dehousse, Renaud. 1992. "Integration versus Regulation? On the Dynamics of Regulation in the European Community." *Journal of Common Market Studies* 30 (December): 383–402.

Department of Foreign Affairs and Trade, Australia. 1988. *Australia–New Zealand Closer Economic Relations Trade Agreement: Documents Arising from the 1988 Review.* Canberra.

Dobson, Wendy. 1991. *Economic Policy Coordination: Requiem or Prologue?* Washington, D.C.: Institute for International Economics.

Dominguez, Kathryn M. 1993. "The Role of International Organizations in the Bretton Woods System." In *A Retrospective on the Bretton Woods System,* edited by Michael D. Bordo and Barry Eichengreen, 357–404. University of Chicago Press.

Drake, William J., and Kalypso Nicolaïdis. 1992. "Ideas, Interests, and Institutionalization: 'Trade in Services' and the Uruguay Round." *International Organization* 46 (Winter): 37–100.

Ehrenberg, Ronald G. 1994. *Labor Markets and Integrating National Economies.* Brookings.

Eichenberg, Richard C., and Russell J. Dalton. 1993. "Europeans and the European Community: The Dynamics of Public Support for European Integration." *International Organization* 47 (Autumn): 507–34.

Eichengreen, Barry. 1989. "Hegemonic Stability Theories of the International Monetary System." In *Can Nations Agree?,* edited by Richard N. Cooper and others, 255–298. Brookings.

Eichengreen, Barry. 1993. "Epilogue: Three Perspectives on the Bretton Woods System." In *A Retrospective on the Bretton Woods System,* edited by Michael D. Bordo and Barry Eichengreen, 621–57. University of Chicago Press.

Eichengreen, Barry. 1994. *International Monetary Arrangements for the 21st Century.* Brookings.

Elster, Jon. 1994. "The Impact of Constitutions on Economic Performance." Paper prepared for the World Bank's Annual Conference on Development Economics. Washington, D.C., April 28–29.

Encarnation, Dennis J. 1992. *Rivals beyond Trade: America versus Japan in Global Competition.* Cornell University Press.

Finlayson, Jock A., and Mark W. Zacher. 1981. "The GATT and the Regulation of Trade Barriers: Regime Dynamics and Functions." *International Organization* 35 (Autumn): 561–602.

Fischer, Stanley. 1988. "International Macroeconomic Policy Coordination." In *International Economic Cooperation,* edited by Martin Feldstein, 11–43. University of Chicago Press.

Flamm, Kenneth. 1990. "Semiconductors." In *Europe 1992: An American Perspective,* edited by Gary Clyde Hufbauer, 225–92. Brookings.

Frankel, Jeffrey A. 1993. "Is Japan Creating a Yen Bloc in East Asia and the Pacific?" In *Regionalism and Rivalry,* edited by Jeffrey A. Frankel and Miles Kahler, 53–85. University of Chicago Press.

Frenkel, Jacob A., Morris Goldstein, and Paul R. Masson. 1991. "Characteristics of a Successful Exchange Rate System." Occasional Paper 82. Washington, D.C.: International Monetary Fund.

Fried, Jonathan T. 1991. "Forum: Binational Dispute Resolution Procedures under the Canada–United States Free Trade Agreement: Experiences to Date and Portents for the Future." *New York University Journal of International Law and Politics* 24 (Fall): 380–82.

Frieden, Jeffry A. 1993. "Economic Liberalization and the Politics of European Monetary Integration." Paper prepared for the Social Science Research Council Project on Foreign Policy Consequences on Economic and Political Liberalization (June).

Funabashi, Yoichi. 1988. *Managing the Dollar: From the Plaza to the Louvre.* Washington, D.C.: Institute for International Economics.

Garrett, Geoffrey. Forthcoming. "Capital Mobility, Trade and the Domestic Politics of Economy Policy." *International Organization.*

General Agreement on Tariffs and Trade. 1994. *The Results of the Uruguay Round of Multilateral Trade Negotiations: The Legal Texts.* Geneva.

Goldstein, Judith, and Robert O. Keohane, eds. 1993. *Ideas and Foreign Policy: Beliefs, Institutions, and Political Change.* Cornell University Press.

Graham, Edward R., and Paul R. Krugman. 1990. "Trade-Related Investment Measures." In *Completing the Uruguay Round,* edited by Jeffrey J. Schott, 153–56. Washington, D.C.: Institute for International Economics.

Haas, Ernest B. 1964. *Beyond the Nation State: Functionalism and International Organization.* Stanford University Press.

Haas, Peter M. 1992. "Introduction: Epistemic Communities and International Policy Coordination." *International Organization* 46 (Winter): 1–35.

Haas, Peter M., Robert O. Keohane, and Marc A. Levy, eds. 1993. *Institutions for the Earth: Sources of Effective International Environmental Protection.* MIT Press.

Haggard, Stephan, and Beth A. Simmons. 1987. "Theories of International Regimes." *International Organization* 41 (Summer): 491–517.

Hamilton, Colleen, and John Whalley. 1988. "Coalitions in the Uruguay Round." Working Paper 2751. Cambridge, Mass.: National Bureau of Economic Research.

Hansson, Göte. 1990. *Harmonization and International Trade.* New York: Routledge.

Herring, Richard J., and Robert E. Litan. 1995. *Financial Regulation in the Global Economy.* Brookings.

Higgott, Richard A., and Andrew Fenton Cooper. 1990. "Middle Power Leadership and Coalition Building: Australia, the Cairns Group and the Uruguay Round of Trade Negotiations." *International Organization* 44 (Autumn): 589–632.

Hilf, Meinhard. 1990. "EC and GATT: A European Proposal for Strengthening the GATT Dispute Settlement Procedures." In *GATT and Conflict Management,* edited by Reinhard Rode, 63–101. Boulder, Colo.: Westview.

Hindley, Brian. 1990. "Services." In *Completing the Uruguay Round,* edited by Jeffrey J. Schott, 130–46. Washington, D.C.: Institute for International Economics.

Hoekman, Bernard M. 1993. "Multilateral Trade Negotiations and Coordination of Commercial Policies." In *The Multilateral Trading System: Analysis and Op-*

tions for Change, edited by Robert M. Stern, 29–62. University of Michigan Press.

Hoekman, Bernard M., and Robert M. Stern. 1993. "An Assessment of the Tokyo Round Agreements and Arrangements." In *The Multilateral Trading System: Analysis and Options for Change*, edited by Robert M. Stern, 63–86. University of Michigan Press.

Hoffmann, Stanley, and Robert O. Keohane, eds. 1991. *The New European Community: Decisionmaking and Institutional Change*. Boulder, Colo.: Westview.

Holtham, Gerald. 1989. "German Macroeconomic Policy and the 1978 Bonn Summit." In *Can Nations Agree?*, edited by Richard N. Cooper and others, 141–77. Brookings.

Hudec, Robert E. 1987. *Developing Countries in the GATT Legal System*. London: Trade Policy Research Centre.

————. 1990. "Dispute Settlement." In *Completing the Uruguay Round*, edited by Jeffrey J. Schott, 180–204. Washington, D.C.: Institute for International Economics.

Hudec, Robert E., Daniel L. M. Kennedy, and Mark Sgarbossa. 1993. "A Statistical Profile of GATT Dispute Settlement Cases: 1948–1989." *Minnesota Journal of Global Trade* 2 (Winter): 1–114.

Hufbauer, Gary Clyde. 1990. "An Overview." In *Europe 1992: An American Perspective*, edited by Gary Clyde Hufbauer, 1–64. Brookings.

Hufbauer, Gary Clyde, and Jeffrey J. Schott. 1993. *NAFTA: An Assessment*. Washington, D.C.: Institute for International Economics.

Jackson, John H. 1984. "Perspectives on the Jurisprudence of International Trade: Costs and Benefits of Legal Procedures in the United States." *Michigan Law Review* 82 (April-May): 1570–87.

————. 1990. *Restructuring the GATT System*. New York: Council on Foreign Relations Press.

————. 1992. *The World Trading System: Law and Policy of International Economic Relations*. MIT Press.

Johnson, Harry G. 1972. *Aspects of the Theory of Tariffs*. Harvard University Press.

Kahler, Miles. 1988. "Organization and Cooperation: International Institutions and Policy Coordination." *Journal of Public Policy* 8 (July-December): 375–401.

————. 1992. "External Influence, Conditionality, and the Politics of Adjustment." In *The Politics of Economic Adjustment*, edited by Stephan Haggard and Robert R. Kaufman, 89–136. Princeton University Press.

————. 1993. "Multilateralism with Small and Large Numbers." In *Multilateralism Matters*, edited by John Gerard Ruggie, 295–326. Columbia University Press.

Kapstein, Ethan B. 1991. "Supervising International Banks: Origins and Implications of the Basle Accord." Essays in International Finance 185. International Finance Section, Department of Economics, Princeton University.

————. 1992. "Between Power and Purpose: Central Bankers and the Politics of Regulatory Convergence." *International Organization* 46 (Winter): 265–88.

Kelmar, Patricia. 1993. "Binational Panels of the Canada–United States Free Trade Agreement in Action: The Constitutional Challenge Continues." *George Washington Journal of Internatonal Law and Economics* 27 (Fall): 173–208.

Keohane, Robert O. 1984. *After Hegemony: Cooperation and Discord in the World Political Economy.* Princeton University Press.

———. 1988. "International Institutions: Two Approaches." *International Studies Quarterly* 32: 379–96.

———. 1989. "Neoliberal Institutionalism: A Perspective on World Politics." In *International Institutions and State Power,* edited by Robert O. Keohane, 1–20. Boulder, Colo.: Westview.

Keohane, Robert, Michael McGinnis, and Elinor Ostrom, eds. 1993. *Proceedings of the Conference on Linking Local and Global Commons Held at Harvard University, April 23–25, 1992.* Cambridge: Harvard University, Center for International Affairs.

King, Gary, Robert O. Keohane, and Sidney Verba. 1994. *Designing Social Inquiry: Scientific Inference in Qualitative Research.* Princeton University Press.

Krasner, Stephen D. 1983. *International Regimes.* Cornell University Press.

Krugman, Paul. 1987. "Is Free Trade Passé?" *Journal of Economic Perspectives* 1 (Fall): 131–44.

———. 1993. "What Do We Need to Know about the International Monetary System?" Essays in International Finance 190. International Finance Section, Department of Economics, Princeton University.

Lange, Peter. 1992. "The Politics of the Social Dimension." In *Euro-politics: Institutions and Policymaking in the "New" European Community,* edited by Alberta M. Sbragia, 225–56. Brookings.

Langhammer, Rolf J., and Ulrich Hiemenz. 1990. *Regional Integration among Developing Countries.* Tübingen: J. C. B. Mohr.

Lawrence, Robert Z. Forthcoming. *Regionalism, Multilateralism, and Deeper Integration.* Brookings.

Lipsey, Richard G., and Murray G. Smith. 1989. "The Canada–U.S. Free Trade Agreement: Special Case or Wave of the Future?" In *Free Trade Areas and U.S. Trade Policy,* edited by Jeffrey J. Schott, 317–36. Washington, D.C.: Institute for International Economics.

Lowenfeld, Andreas F. 1991. "Binational Dispute Settlement under Chapter 19 of the Canada–United States Free Trade Agreement: An Interim Appraisal." *New York University Journal of International Law and Politics* 24 (Fall): 269–339.

———. 1994. "Remedies along with Rights: Institutional Reform in the New GATT." *American Journal of International Law* 88 (July): 477–88.

Ludlow, Peter. 1991. "The European Commission." In *The New European Community,* edited by Stanley Hoffmann and Robert O. Keohane, 85–132. Boulder, Colo.: Westview.

Mancini, G. Federico. 1991. "The Making of a Constitution for Europe." In *The New European Community,* edited by Stanley Hoffmann and Robert O. Keohane, 177–94. Boulder, Colo.: Westview.

Martin, Lisa L. 1993. "The Rational State Choice of Multilateralism." In *Multilateralism Matters,* edited by John Gerard Ruggie, 91–121. Columbia University Press.

Masera, Rainer S., and Robert Triffin, eds. 1984. *Europe's Money: Problems of European Monetary Coordination and Integration.* Oxford: Clarendon Press.

Maskus, Keith E. 1990. "Intellectual Property." In *Completing the Uruguay Round,* edited by Jeffrey J. Schott, 164–79. Washington, D.C.: Institute for International Economics.

Maxfield, Sylvia. 1993. "Financial Liberalization and Regional Monetary Cooperation: The Mexican Case." Paper prepared for the Social Science Research Council Project on Foreign Policy Consequences of Economic and Political Liberalization (June).

McCubbins, Matthew D., and Thomas Schwartz. 1984. "Congressional Oversight Overlooked: Police Patrols versus Fire Alarms." *American Journal of Political Science* 8 (February): 165–79.

McKibbin, Warwick J., and Jeffrey D. Sachs. 1991. *Global Linkages: Macroeconomic Interdependence and Cooperation in the World Economy.* Brookings.

Milgrom, Paul, and John Roberts. 1990. "Bargaining Costs, Influence Costs, and the Organization of Economic Activity." In *Perspectives on Positive Political Economy,* edited by James E. Alt and Kenneth A. Shepsle, 57–89. Cambridge University Press.

Mora, Miguel Montana I. 1993. "A GATT with Teeth: Law Wins over Politics in the Resolution of International Trade Disputes." *Columbia Journal of International Law* 31 (1): 103–80.

Mosley, Paul. 1987. "Conditionality as Bargaining Process: Structural Adjustment Lending, 1980–86." Essays in International Finance 168. International Finance Section, Department of Economics, Princeton University.

Mosley, Paul, Jane Harrigan, and John Toye. 1991. *Aid and Power: The World Bank and Policy-Based Lending.* London: Routledge.

Nivola, Pietro S.. 1993. *Regulating Unfair Trade.* Brookings.

Nugent, Neill. 1992. "The Deepening and Widening of the European Community." *Journal of Common Market Studies* 30 (September): 311–28.

Ostrom, Elinor. 1990. *Governing the Commons: The Evolution of Institutions for Collective Action.* Cambridge University Press.

Ostrom, Elinor, James Walker, and Roy Gardner. 1992. "Covenants with and without a Sword: Self-Governance Is Possible." *American Political Science Review* 86 (June): 404–17.

Ostry, Sylvia. 1990. *Governments and Corporations in a Shrinking World: Trade and Innovation Policies in the United States, Europe and Japan.* New York: Council on Foreign Relations Press.

Oudiz, Gilles, and Jeffrey Sachs. 1984. "Macroeconomic Policy Coordination among the Industrial Economies." *Brookings Papers on Economic Activity* 1: 1–65.

Oye, Kenneth A. 1985. "Explaining Cooperation under Anarchy: Hypotheses and Strategies." *World Politics* 38 (October): 1–24.

———. 1992. *Economic Discrimination and Political Exchange: The World Political Economy in the 1930s and 1980s.* Princeton University Press.

Palmeter, David. 1993. "Environment and Trade: Much Ado about Little?" *Journal of World Trade* 27 (June): 55–70.

Patterson, Gardener. 1966. *Discrimination in International Trade: The Policy Issues, 1945–1965.* Princeton University Press.

Pauly, Louis W. 1992. "The Political Foundations of Multilateral Economic Surveillance." *International Journal* 47 (Spring): 293–327.

Pelkmans, Jacques. 1987. "The New Approach to Technical Harmonization and Standardization." *Journal of Common Market Studies* 25 (March): 249–69.

Pescatore, Pierre. 1993. "The GATT Dispute Settlement Mechanism: Its Present Situation and Its Prospects." *Journal of World Trade* 27 (February): 5–20.

Petersmann, Ernst-Ulrich. 1993. "International Trade Law and International Environmental Law: Prevention and Settlement of Internatonal Environmental Disputes in GATT." *Journal of World Trade* 27 (February): 43–81.

Petri, Peter A. 1993. "The East Asian Trading Bloc." In *Regionalism and Rivalry*, edited by Jeffrey A. Frankel and Miles Kahler, 21–52. University of Chicago Press.

Polak, Jacques J. 1991. "The Changing Nature of IMF Conditionality." Essays in International Finance 184. International Finance Section, Department of Economics, Princeton University.

Price, Victoria Curzon. 1989. "Three Models of European Integration." In *Whose Europe? Competing Visions for 1992*, edited by Sir Ralf Dahrendorf and others, 24–37. London: Institute of Economic Affairs.

———. 1992. "New Institutional Developments in GATT." *Minnesota Journal of Global Trade* 1 (1): 87–110.

Putnam, Robert D., and Nicholas Bayne. 1987. *Hanging Together: Cooperation and Conflict in the Seven Power Summits*, rev. ed. London: Sage.

Putnam, Robert D., and C. Randall Henning. 1989. "The Bonn Summit of 1978: A Case Study in Coordination." In *Can Nations Agree?*, edited by Richard N. Cooper and others, 12–140. Brookings.

Reder, Melvin, and Lloyd Ulman. 1993. "Unionism and Unification." In *Labor and an Integrated Europe*, edited by Lloyd Ulman, Barry Eichengreen, and William T. Dickens, 13–44. Brookings.

Richardson, J. David. 1988. "International Coordination of Trade Policy." In *International Economic Cooperation*, edited by Martin Feldstein, 167–204. University of Chicago Press.

———. 1993. "East Asian Problem." In *Pacific Economic Relations in the 1990s*, edited by Richard Higgott, Richard Leaver, and John Ravenhill, 102–185. Boulder, Colo.: Westview.

Robson, Peter. 1987. *The Economics of International Integration*, 3rd rev. ed. Boston: Allen & Unwin.

Rode, Reinhard, ed. 1990. *GATT and Conflict Management: A Transatlantic Strategy for a Stronger Regime.* Boulder, Colo.: Westview.

Rostow, W. W. 1986. *The United States and the Regional Organization of Asia and the Pacific, 1965–1985.* University of Texas Press.

Ruggie, John Gerard, ed. 1993a. *Multilateralism Matters: The Theory and Praxis of an Institutional Form.* Columbia University Press.

———. 1993b. "Territoriality and Beyond: Problematizing Modernity in International Relations." *International Organization* 47 (Winter): 139–74.

Sachs, Jeffrey D. 1988. "International Policy Coordination: The Case of the Developing Country Debt Crisis." In *International Economic Cooperation,* edited by Martin Feldstein, 233–78. University of Chicago Press.

Sbragia, Alberta M., ed. 1992. *Euro-politics: Institutions and Policymaking in the "New" European Community.* Brookings.

Scott, Hal S., and Shinsaku Iwahara. 1994. *In Search of a Level Playing Field: The Implementation of the Basle Capital Accord in Japan and the United States.* Washington, D.C.: Group of Thirty Publications.

Shapiro, Martin M. 1981. *Courts: A Comparative and Political Analysis.* University of Chicago Press.

———. 1992. "The European Court of Justice." In *The New European Community,* edited by Alberta M. Sbragia, 123–56. Brookings.

Shklar, Judith. 1964. *Legalism.* Cambridge: Harvard University Press.

Snidal, Duncan. 1985. "Coordination versus Prisoner's Dilemma: Implications for International Cooperation and Regimes." *American Political Science Review* 79 (December): 923–42.

Sorsa, Piritta. 1992. "The Environment: A New Challenge to GATT?" World Bank Policy Research Working Paper 980 (September).

Stein, Arthur A. 1990. *Why Nations Cooperate: Circumstance and Choice in International Relations.* Cornell University Press.

Steinberg, Richard H. 1994. "The Uruguay Round: A Legal Analysis of the Final Act." *International Quarterly* 6 (April): 1–97.

Streeck, Wolfgang. 1993. "The Rise and Decline of Neocorporatism." In *Labor and an Integrated Europe,* edited by Lloyd Ulman, Barry Eichengreen, and William T. Dickens, 80–99. Brookings.

Sugden, Robert. 1986. *The Economics of Rights, Co-operation and Welfare.* Oxford: Basil Blackwell Ltd.

Sykes, Alan O. 1995. *Product Standards for Internationally Integrated Goods Markets.* Brookings.

Thomson, Graeme, and Christopher Langman. 1991. "The Removal of Trade Remedy Law in Trans-Tasman Commerce." *Canada–United States Law Journal* 17 (1): 203–7.

Torre, Augusto de la, and Margaret R. Kelly. 1992. "Regional Trade Arrangements." Occasional Paper 93. Washington, D.C.: International Monetary Fund.

Trachtman, Joel P. 1992. "GATT Dispute Settlement Panel: United States—Restrictions on Imports of Tuna." *American Journal of International Law* 86 (January): 142–51.

Turner, Lowell. 1993. "Prospects for Worker Participation in Management in the Single Market." In *Labor and an Integrated Europe,* edited by Lloyd Ulman, Barry Eichengreen, and William T. Dickens, 45–79. Brookings.

Weatherford, M. Stephen. 1988. "The International Economy as a Constraint on U.S. Macroeconomic Policymaking." *International Organization* 42 (Autumn): 605–38.

Wessels, Wolfgang. 1991a. "Administrative Interaction." In *The Dynamics of European Integration,* edited by William Wallace, 229–41. London: Pinter.

———. 1991b. "The EC Council: The Community's Decisionmaking Center." In *The New European Community,* edited by Stanley Hoffmann and Robert O. Keohane, 133–54. Boulder, Colo.: Westview.

Wilkinson, Derrick G. 1994. "NAFTA and the Environment: Some Lessons for the Next Round of GATT Negotiations." *World Economy* 17 (May):395–412.

Williams, Shirley. 1991. "Sovereignty and Accountability in the European Community." In *The New European Community,* edited by Stanley Hoffmann and Robert O. Keohane, 155–76. Boulder, Colo.: Westview.

Williamson, Oliver E. 1985. *The Economic Institutions of Capitalism: Firms, Markets, Relational Contracting.* New York: Free Press.

———. 1994. "Institutions and Economic Organization: The Governance Perspective." Paper prepared for the World Bank's annual conference on development economics. Washington, D.C., April 28–29.

Winham, Gilbert R. 1986. *International Trade and the Tokyo Round Negotiation.* Princeton University Press.

———. 1989. "The Prenegotiation Phase of the Uruguay Round." In *Getting to the Table: The Processes of International Prenegotiation,* edited by Janice Gross Stein. Johns Hopkins University Press.

———. 1992. *The Evolution of International Trade Agreements.* University of Toronto Press.

Yarbrough, Beth V., and Robert M. Yarbrough. 1992. *Cooperation and Governance in International Trade: The Strategic Organizational Approach.* Princeton University Press.

Zamora, Stephen. 1993. "The Americanization of Mexican Law: Non-Trade Issues in the North American Free Trade Agreement." *Law and Policy in International Business* 24 (Winter): 391–459.

Index